Hunting Predators

Proven Tactics That Work

Hunting Wisdom Library

NORTH★AMERICAN★HUNTING★CLUB

MINNETONKA, MINNESOTA

About the Author

Gordy Krahn grew up in the Northwoods of Minnesota and has spent a lifetime hunting and trapping the fields, marshes and forests of the North. Former editor of the *Trapper & Predator Caller* magazine, Gordy has pursued predators north, south, east and west and has produced three instructional videos and written innumerable articles on how to call predators sure-kill close. Gordy is currently Editor of *North American Hunter*.

About the Primary Photographer

Mark S. Werner Sr. has been a wildlife photographer since 1984. Born in the Upper Peninsula of Michigan, he grew up along the Menominee River in northeastern Wisconsin. As a young trapper and predator caller, Mark developed the skills necessary for success with both rifle and camera. Today, his images, along with his wife Sue's, appear regularly in regional and national magazines, calendars and postcards. Mark and Sue also operate a complete limited edition wildlife print business.

HUNTING PREDATORS
Proven Tactics That Work

Printed in 2006.

Tom Carpenter
Creative Director

Heather Koshiol
Senior Book Development Coordinator

Shari Gross
Book Development Assistant

7 8 9 10 / 08 07 06
ISBN 1-58159-110-1
© 2001 North American Hunting Club

North American Hunting Club
12301 Whitewater Drive
Minnetonka, MN 55343
www.huntingclub.com

PHOTO CREDITS

All photography by **Mark Werner** except:
Gerry Blair: 12 (left), 12 (bottom right); **Tim Christie:** 4; **Judd Cooney:** 76, 102, 145 (left); **Mike Faw:** 46 (top); **Joe Goodman:** 153 (all), 154 (all), 155 (all); **Gregg Gutchow:** 6; **Donald Jones:** 23 (top), 33, 27 (both), 58, 145 (right); **Mark Kayser:** 3, 18, 21 (bottom), 23 (bottom), 50, 78, 83, 86, 87 (bottom), 106, 118, 122 (top), 121 (both), 124; **Gordy Krahn (NAHC):** 1 (both), 10 (both), 15, 16, 17 (bottom), 32, 36, 37 (bottom), 39, 41, 44, 47, 48, 49 (bottom), 51 (all), 52, 53 (all), 54 (right), 59, 61 (top), 63 (top), 64, 66, 69, 72, 74, 82, 84 (bottom), 87 (top), 90 (both), 93, 94, 95, 96 (top), 98, 100, 101, 104 (bottom), 105, 107, 110, 111 (bottom), 112 (top), 114 (top), 120 (bottom), 128, 131 (both), 132 (bottom), 135 (top), 137 (top), 142, 148 (both), 152; **Gary Kramer:** 49 (bottom), 132 (top), 134, 135 (bottom); **Bill Marchel:** cover, 21 (top), 65, 84 (top), 88, 89 (bottom), 96 (bottom), 97, 112 (bottom), 129 (top), 137 (bottom); **Wyman Meinzer:** 60, 61 (bottom), 85 (bottom); **Wyman Meinzer/GS:** 56, 57 (all), 67, 70 (both), 103 (bottom), 108 (bottom), 126 (bottom); **John Muegge:** 31; **Bob Noonan:** 16 (bottom), 150, 156, 157; **Gerald Stewart:** 12 (top right), 13, 14, 55 (top), 77 (both), 79; **Bryce Towsley:** 2, 37 (top), 38, 40, 42 (both), 45 (left), 46 (bottom), 75, 103 (top), 104 (top), 120 (top), 126 (top); **Bill Vaznis/The Green Agency:** 146 (bottom).

Special thanks to

for the use of several images in this book. Call 1-800-258-0929 (code ABA2AI) for subscription information.

Table of Contents

Foreword

What is the ultimate game animal? The answer lies in the preferences and experiences of the individual hunter. But we all certainly agree on parts of the definition.

The ultimate game must be crafty and cautious. It must have extremely acute senses. It must inhabit a wide range of habitat and terrain.

The ultimate game animal should provide wide opportunity for human hunters. It should require some level of physical challenge to hunt. It should be a difficult target whether the hunting tool is rifle, handgun, shotgun, muzzleloader or bow and arrow. The season should be long and the rewards for success high. It should offer a complete hunting challenge including woods lore, concealment, calling and tracking.

Many animals fit one or several of these specifications. Few fulfill them all. One that does is likely readily available to you to hunt, yet is one that you may never have specifically pursued.

It's the coyote!

Longtime North American Hunting Club member and handgunning expert Hal Swiggett hunted his way around the world several times—pursuing all sorts of North American and African game and hunting in the company of royalty. He did it all. And that diversity of hunting experience led Hal to the conclusion that predators of all kinds—and particularly the coyote—are the world's greatest hunting challenges!

So it is high time the North American Hunting Club created a book on the pursuit of the pursuers. And as usual, we've come up with the best!

Author Gordy Krahn is one of those rare individuals who knows the way of foxes, bobcats, coyotes and other predators—all creatures worthy of the title "ultimate game animal!" Gordy has trapped them and hunted them, both in his own tracks as well as in the snowshoe prints of the best predator hunters and trappers on the continent.

We're fortunate to have Gordy as Editor of *North American Hunter* magazine. You're fortunate to have a book in your hands that comes from a guy like Gordy. To him, pursuing the pursuers is a way of life.

Sure, like most of us NAHC members, Gordy hunts about all that there is to be hunted. But his specialty—his passion—is hunting predators. He is a storehouse of secrets that are dying with the old-time predator hunters and trappers. Here's your chance to glean those strategies, techniques and tips.

If you hunt predators already, this book will make you even better. If you haven't sampled the ultimate hunting challenge, it's time to give it a try. It's fun, it's available almost everywhere. And its rewards must be experienced to be understood. It's time to get hooked.

Best afield,

Bill

Bill Miller
Executive Director — North American Hunting Club

INTRODUCTION

I froze in my tracks as I stepped into a clearing dissecting a white birch ridge that glimmered like a fresh oil painting in the dim morning light. A flash of red fur on the clearing's opposite side had triggered an age-old response. I silently dropped to the ground and slid behind a moss-covered log, grouse gun tucked close by my side. Slowly, I raised my head and watched a large male fox, oblivious to my presence, intently working the dry grass and fallen leaves for rodents, insects or whatever other groceries he could rustle up.

Easing back behind the log, I emitted a soft squeak between pursed lips. The fox snapped erect, his attention directed toward my location. Another coaxing squeal had him doing the fox trot, closing the ground between us.

Seconds later, I heard his footfalls as he approached the log that separated us. I had no intention of shooting. Autumn was in its early stages and fur was far from prime. I had a strong hankering, however, to trick the fabled trickster, and he was falling for the oldest ruse in the book ... hook, line and sinker.

I held my breath as the fox placed his front paws on the log and cautiously peered over the top, head cocked to one side. Our eyes locked and we both involuntarily jolted, uncomfortable with the abrupt invasion of personal space. The fox nearly turned himself inside out trying to put some ground between us, but suddenly slid to a halt not 30 yards away. He turned around and gave me a lasting, sly look, as if to say, "You won't get me with that next time." Then he turned and melted into the golden forest.

That experience more than 25 years ago in northern Minnesota set the hook. And the thrill of that moment, and so many others that have followed over the years, transformed an otherwise "normal" outdoorsman into a predator-hunting fanatic. My passion to hunt predators has taken me to the high deserts of Arizona, the vast range lands of Texas, Midwestern prairies, and all other points of the compass. I have shared the company of some of the best hunting buddies a guy could hope for—Gerry Blair, Gerald Stewart, Larry O. Gates, Major Boddicker, Mark Miller, Scott Huber and John Graham, to name a few.

This book is dedicated to those individuals, both east and west of the big river, who have the gumption to brazen out adverse conditions and match wits with nature's most cunning adversaries—hunting the hunters, stalking the stalkers. I'm betting the pages that follow will help inspire and motivate you to be a better predator hunter ... or maybe even take up the addiction!

So sit back, turn the pages and enjoy. I truly hope that each chapter puts an itch in your trigger finger and sparks a desire to dust off your hunting gear and take to the field for a glimpse of that elusive flash of fur.

Chapter One

THE EVOLUTION OF PREDATOR HUNTING

When prehistoric men embarked on the hunt in search of food, they did so as predators in every sense of the word. They didn't hunt for sport—although they might have enjoyed matching wits with their prey. Rather, they hunted to survive in an extremely harsh and dangerous environment. Animals provided sustenance, as well as skins for clothing and bones for making tools.

Prehistoric man's limited physical "tools" required that he hunt on a more cerebral level than other animals; but basically these early humans were predators, not unlike the wolves, lions and bears that they competed with for local food sources.

Early man learned the value of using animal sounds and other trickery to lure his prey close for the kill: imitating the plaintive bleats of fawn deer to draw an anxious doe near; making squeaking sounds to lure curious muskrats close; mimicking the mating sounds of wild turkeys and other birds to draw them near. All served the goal of obtaining food.

Early on, man must have realized that many of these sounds drew the interest of other predators. And since these animals were also considered a source of food and clothing—as well as competition for other food sources—early man became a hunter of other predators.

So our predatory roots run deep. And while hunting predators has evolved from survival to sport, many elements of the hunt have remained remarkably unchanged since the days of prehistoric man. Our inherent drive to hunt, to compete, to match wits with other predators is as timeless as the pursuit itself.

THE EARLY YEARS

odern-day predator hunting grew out of the West. As pioneers pushed westward, chasing their precious hopes and dreams, they carved out an existence in an often harsh and challenging environment. Armed with farming and ranching skills, pioneers attempted to tame a frontier that was considered wild and was unsettled by Europeans.

Making a living was tough during pioneer days, and when predators competed for wild game and preyed on domestic livestock, the simple remedy was to eliminate the problem. Predators like wolves, coyotes, bobcats, mountain lions—practically any critter with fur and sharp teeth—were considered the enemy.

The wolf, the grizzly bear, the mountain lion—all felt the wrath of man as he pushed civilization westward, determined to see what lay beyond the next expanse of prairie or rugged mountain range. As frontier hunters cut deep into their food sources, the large predators were pushed to the brink of extinction; they suffered further losses by frontiersmen who relentlessly trapped and hunted them.

GOVERNMENT PREDATOR CONTROL EFFORTS

Early on, the government got into the business of predator control. In 1909, Congress appropriated money for the U.S. Department of Agriculture's (USDA) Biological Survey Division to research means of controlling animals harmful to agriculture. The Branch of Predator and Rodent Control (PARC) was created within the USDA's Biological Service Office to carry out that purpose and encourage settlement of the West by opening the land to livestock and farming.

In 1931, Congress passed the Animal Damage Control (ADC) Act, which authorized

Animal damage control agents and private fur trappers help keep predator numbers in balance with their habitats.

the control of wild animals that caused injury to agriculture, horticulture, forestry, animal husbandry, wildlife and birds. Aimed at general population reduction, these early efforts to control predator populations were extremely effective. More recently, however, ADC efforts are directed at removing individual nuisance animals and even nonlethal methods of control (prevention) in some cases.

Fur Market

The value of fur has historically provided a check and balance for keeping predator populations manageable and has worked in tandem with government controls. Historically, when fur prices have been favorable, private trappers and fur hunters were capable of controlling the populations of furbearing animals.

It is when fur prices are down that predator populations are difficult to manage, and damage to both wildlife and domestic livestock increases. Government agencies typically do not have the funding or the manpower to effectively control predator populations without the aid of private fur harvesters.

Coyotes, in particular, have long been one of the most controversial of all nongame animals. Agricultural entities have urged coyote control by whatever means necessary, so that actual and potential livestock losses may be eliminated. As an example, since 1891, when the first programs aimed at control were begun in California, nearly 500,000 coyotes have been reported destroyed at a cost of an estimated $30 million of the taxpayers' money.

Earliest predator control efforts were carried out by ADC men—those working for the government and private ranches and farms. Most were trappers, but they also employed calling tactics, especially when faced with trap-shy animals. They used hand-fashioned calls and even their own voices to call and kill depredating coyotes.

Where Are We Headed?

Many environmentalists believe that predators are necessary to preserve the delicate balance of nature and must be protected.

Some hunters think that predators are responsible for declines in game species and that predator populations should be reduced.

Biologists agree that individual animals preying on livestock and poultry should be destroyed but that predator species as a whole are not necessarily harmful, because much of their diet is made up of destructive rodents. Biologists also point to studies showing that predators have no lasting detrimental effects on other wildlife populations.

These arguments, as well as control efforts, have changed very little in the past 100 years: Hunting and trapping continue to be the primary tools for controlling predators. In many parts of the West, predator populations are presently high due to low fur prices and the inability of government agencies to control predator populations on their own due to a lack of funding and manpower.

Coyotes have recently been classified as nongame animals in many states and may be taken throughout the year by those possessing valid hunting licenses. Other predators are listed as game animals or furbearers, and their harvest is regulated.

The control of predators continues to be a necessary part of maintaining an equilibrium in which man's presence cannot be denied. Protecting livestock and game species from coyotes, foxes, bobcats and other predators, for the benefit of man, will continue to be an important part of predator control work; as always, the price of fur will also continue to factor into predator-harvesting efforts.

Left unchecked, predators can do considerable damage to other wildlife species and domestic livestock.

THE PIONEERS

Clockwise from left: J. Murray Burnham, Johnny Stewart (at right) and A. L. Lindsey ushered in the modern predator hunting era.

We owe a lot to a few visionary hunters from the 1940s, '50s and '60s who developed the predator-calling industry that we enjoy today. They were an intrepid lot, dedicated to their sport with a passion that bordered fanaticism.

Traditionally, trapping and hunting methods were mired in secrecy. Information was disseminated among family members and close friends and rarely were secrets shared outside of small social circles.

J. Murray Burnham, Dwight Thomas, A.L. Lindsey, Wayne Weems, Johnny Stewart and others changed that. They shared their predator hunting knowledge and skills with those new to the sport, and developed and sold products to make time in the field more productive. Many of the calling devices that are in use today still proudly display the names of these predator-hunting pioneers.

While it would be impossible to detail here the complete evolution of predator hunting that followed World War II, or to mention all of those who contributed to that growth, there are names that need mentioning.

J. MURRAY BURNHAM

J. Murray Burnham is acknowledged by many as the father of modern predator calling. As a youngster, Burnham observed a screaming rabbit that was caught in a fence and was then attacked and eaten by wolves. He quickly realized that the sounds of the rabbit in distress were what had attracted the canines, so he practiced making the sounds with his mouth.

The Johnny Stewart Call Company

Of all the founding fathers of the modern predator hunting era, the late Johnny Stewart probably had the most lasting effect on the industry. In fact, the Stewart name is practically synonymous with the sport of predator calling. Johnny's love of the outdoors and his passion for hunting predators produced a legacy that has survived nearly four decades.

The Johnny Stewart Wildlife Call Company was founded in 1961 in Waco, Texas. It marketed phonographs and recorded animal sounds on 45 rpm records in the earliest days. Eight-track players and tapes came along in the mid-'60s, and the cassette players and tapes that are still sold today were introduced in 1972.

Perhaps even more important than the development of electronic game callers were Johnny's recordings of actual wild animal sounds for which he set a standard of excellence. Even today, the quality of the sounds that he recorded back in the 1960s and '70s is unsurpassed.

Throughout the 1960s, Johnny tirelessly promoted the sport of predator calling through seminars and advertising. He traveled across the country showing films of animals responding to his recorded sounds. In some states he also participated in blocking the introduction of legislation that would have prohibited the activity. He was instrumental in educating hunters on all the aspects of calling wildlife.

But in those early years, even though the industry was still very undeveloped, there were several regional and national companies hot on Johnny's trail. In fact, Burnham Brothers Calls, established in 1954, was the largest commercial call manufacturer at that time. Many companies were selling records and record players, and some offered mouth-

Johnny Stewart saw a need to educate and equip those new to the sport of predator hunting, and in 1961 founded the Johnny Stewart Wildlife Call Company.

blown calls. They provided recordings of domestic animals and recordings of people making animal sounds with mouth-blown calls. Johnny always believed that he was the first to record the actual distress sounds of wild rabbits. And it was almost by accident that he got the idea.

One night, a raccoon sneaked into the Stewarts' backyard and killed a pet chicken. The sounds of that dying chicken left an impression on Johnny and initiated the development of the most comprehensive line of wildlife calling sounds to date. His friends thought he was crazy to think he could make a living selling animal recordings.

Johnny Stewart passed away in 1987, and his son, Gerald Stewart, succeeded him as president of the company. For the next 12 years, Gerald met the needs of a new generation of predator callers, continuing to develop new products while improving on the old.

Continued ...

The Johnny Stewart Call Company *continued*

In November 1999, the company was sold to Hunter's Specialties, which continues to market the entire line of Johnny Stewart products.

"Our dominant position in a rapidly growing market made us a desirable acquisition by the largest supplier of hunting accessories in the industry," Gerald Stewart said. "Joining forces with a company with greater marketing resources and aggressiveness will keep us dominant for many years to come."

Johnny Stewart spent countless hours in the field experimenting with animal recordings and developing new products for predator hunters.

Utilizing this new skill, Burnham earned a reputation as a proficient predator hunter. After World War II, Murray and his brother, Winston, began Burnham Brothers Company and developed and marketed an extensive line of predator calls. Many believe that he developed the first mouth-blown predator call.

DWIGHT THOMAS

Dwight Thomas began experimenting with calling coyotes in the 1920s. He observed that coyotes came to the sound of a call and circled downwind for their final approach. He also experimented with ladders and elevated stands, noting that predators rarely look up when drawing near the call. Dwight experimented with many materials, including blades of grass, strips of paper, cow horns and combs.

In 1955, Dwight developed his first call, the Model 141, which he turned on a Delta lathe with a duplicator. In 1971, Dwight started turning out his calls on a production lathe at a rate of 10,000 calls per year.

Thomas predator calls were mostly made of high-quality walnut until 1975, when he began making his calls out of plastic.

A. L. LINDSEY

Adam Lynn Lindsey, a Texan, turned out his first predator call, fashioned from a cow horn, in 1949. Shortly after that, he began marketing them. After selecting the horns, he would submerge them in boil-ing water to soften them. The next step was to clear an air passage and file them to the proper thickness.

He used steel wool to finish the insides of the horns, and each horn received a generous buffing on the outside. The inner workings consisted of a brass reed mounted on one-half of a copper jacket of a .30-caliber bullet that was split in half lengthwise. Waxed thread was wrapped around the pieces until the sound was correct.

Lindsey marketed his calls by showing local ranchers how to call foxes, wolves and bobcats. These men dubbed him the "Modern Pied Piper," a name which his calls carried.

As demand for his calls increased, he began fashioning them from plastic in 1951.

The last call to carry the Pied Piper name was called the Long Range, which was made in 1955.

OTHER NAMES

There were others. Jack Cain and Lew Mossinger of Arizona designed and marketed the Circe line of calls now owned by Lohman Game Calls. Wayne Weems developed the famous Weems Wild Call line of hand calls. Johnny Stewart developed a complete line of hand and electronic game calls.

These men, and many others who followed in their footsteps, provided accessibility to the sport of predator calling. It was through their vision and initiative that the evolution of predator hunting as we know it today unfolded.

PREDATOR HUNTING— A GROWING SPORT

From its meager beginnings, predator hunting—and the cottage industry that supports it—has developed into a multimillion-dollar enterprise and has experienced considerable growth and prosperity in the past five decades.

More and more sportsmen are extending their hunting seasons deep into the winter months and that has translated into profit for those companies, big and small, that specialize in the products varminteers tote into the field. Guns and ammunition, camouflage clothing, predator calls (both electronic and hand-held), shooting sticks and bipods, spotlights—the list goes on and on.

But even in recent history the sport of collecting fur has been a cyclic roller coaster ride. Fluctuations in the fur market have periodically affected both hunter and predator, as well as the companies that depend on participation and recruitment into the sport.

THE FUR BOOM

Without question, the fur boom of the 1970s and 1980s contributed to the growth of the predator hunting industry. Harvesting fur was profitable, and manufacturers saw the opportunity to peddle products to hunters eager to increase efficiency and profit afield. It was easy for hunters of that era to justify equipment expenditures—the purchase of a cassette machine that cost a couple hundred bucks or even a semi-new 4-wheel-drive truck—because the profit made from harvesting fur would go a long way toward footing the bill for new gear. Some trappers and fur hunters were even traveling from state to state in search of valuable fur.

THE MARKET CRASH OF 1987

But if the fur market is anything, it's fickle, and the joyride came abruptly to a halt in 1987 when the industry experienced one of its deepest declines in

The Evolution of Predator Hunting

When it became less profitable to harvest fur in the late 1980s and early 1990s, animal damage control agents and private fur hunters displaced trappers as primary predator-control agents.

decades. Coyote pelts that averaged $35 in 1982 were practically worthless by the end of that decade. And the national harvest dropped from more than 420,000 coyotes in 1982 to 158,000 by 1992, when the average price paid for coyote pelts had declined to $13. And the number of fur harvesters in the field, both hunters and trappers, declined as well. The money simply wasn't there to interest those whose sole purpose in pursuing furbearers was profit.

In some ways, this was good news for hunters dedicated to the sport of calling predators—it meant more animals and less competition. Predator populations increased and ranchers and farmers welcomed hunters to solve their depredation problems. Those interested in hunting for sport accepted the lower profit margins ... and enjoyed the best of times for hunting predators.

As this book goes to press, fur prices are apparently rebounding to some degree, most likely the result of a diminished harvest and increased demand. At the North American Fur Auction in Canada recently, Western coyotes—those preferred pales with white bellies—brought an average of $32.62 and, even more encouraging, 98 percent of those coyotes offered at the sale were sold. Even the less desirable Eastern coyotes brought an average of better than $20. Red foxes sold at an average of about $16.

Only time will tell if this is a bump in the road or if it is a trend toward increasing fur prices. But it is encouraging to see that there continues to be a viable market and a demand for the furs we harvest.

CHANGING OF THE GUARD

When fur prices hit rock bottom, ADC agents and private fur hunters displaced trappers as primary predator-control agents. While dedicated trappers continued to harvest furbearing animals, they did so in greatly diminished numbers.

And, according to the industry experts, interest in predator hunting is at an all-time high and there is no indication of a slowdown. According to Gerald Stewart, sales of his company's electronic callers and tapes has grown 300 percent since the late 1980s and 1,500 percent since the 1960s. And this is in the face of increased competition as other companies, new and established, compete for market share. Gerald estimates a $5- to $6-million-a-year industry on the electronics portion alone.

POPULATION CONTROL

Trapping and fur hunting will continue to be the most viable means of dealing with predator problems and for keeping predator numbers in check. It would be cost prohibitive for government agencies to manage wildlife populations by relying solely on their

The fur market has experienced a series of ebbs and flows in recent years, but there is still a strong market for wild furs.

own internal resources. Consequently, agencies rely on private hunters and trappers who pay license fees for the privilege of harvesting these animals.

"Bears in the Backyard, Deer in the Driveway," a report prepared by Southwick Associates for the International Association of Fish and Wildlife Agencies, concluded that no amount of additional funding could replace the services provided by trappers and hunters. And research conducted at Utah State University's Jack H. Berryman Institute concluded that if hunting and trapping were removed as control tools, the raccoon population in the Northeast could increase 100 percent and the number of coyotes in the Southeast could increase by 210 percent.

According to the Southwick report: "Hunting and trapping are not the only ways to manage wildlife populations, but are among the most effective methods used by wildlife professionals. If the government had to manage wildlife populations by relying solely on its own internal resources, the cost would be prohibitive. In contrast, many people who hunt or trap recreationally do not have to be paid to provide this service. Instead, hunters and trappers pay for the privilege of hunting and trapping by purchasing licenses from the state and federal governments. The use of hunters and trappers to harvest animals is the most cost-effective way for the government to manage wildlife populations."

Trapping and hunting, the most viable means of predator control, both help ensure that healthy animals exist in a vibrant environment.

The Evolution of Predator Hunting

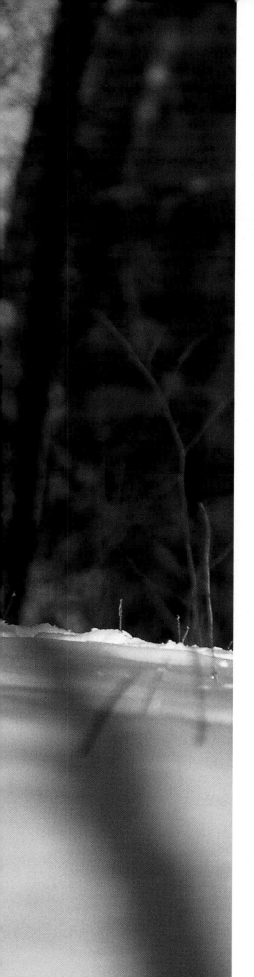

Chapter Two

THE BIOLOGY OF PREDATOR HUNTING

*I*t's called the domino effect—a cumulative consequence produced when one event initiates a succession of other events. They occur both randomly and by design, and are neither inherently good nor bad—they simply exist.

Predator/prey relationships, by design, create codependencies that keep animal populations in balance with their habitats. And in true domino fashion, predator numbers rise in response to increases in prey base and fall when prey species numbers decline. This is nature's equation for equilibrium, needed to sustain healthy animals in a vibrant environment.

The science of predator hunting plays on the relationships between predators and their prey, as well as on intense competition among those predatory species we hunt. Knowing where the rabbit spends the majority of its time, for instance, gives insight to where coyotes, foxes and bobcats hang out and hunt. Predator hunting requires that we hunker in lowly ambush under the pretense that we are prey in distress; or that we mimic the distress cries of predators' young, tugging at parental instincts; or that we use vocalizations to defy social status or play on predators' inherent gregarious nature.

Without a doubt, predator hunting requires that we enter the field with advanced knowledge about the animals we pursue. It is only when we understand what makes these predators tick that we will enjoy optimal success afield.

Playing the predator game will test your hunting and woodsmanship skills to their outer limits. It will challenge your own predatory instincts, and you might be surprised to find that they are thinly veiled. To hunt the ultimate hunter (coyote), trick the supreme trickster (fox), mesmerize the consummate prowler (bobcat), you must learn to think like a canine and move like a feline.

PREDATOR/PREY RELATIONSHIPS

Predators respond to the distress screams of the prey species they hunt because they have to. Competition for food demands it. The more scarce food is, the more fierce the rivalry and competition. And the protein that predators secure by their ability to successfully compete for those resources defines the fine line between prosperity and deficiency. Predators that fail in this quest die and become sustenance for those that have honed their skills.

Of course, this is a simplification of nature's extremely complex predator/prey relationships. Predation in its actions and reactions is more than just a transfer of energy. It represents an interaction between two or more species, between hunters and the hunted. The relative health and prosperity of some predators might depend on the abundance of their prey, and the population of the prey might be controlled by its predators. The symbiotic relationship between the Canada lynx and snowshoe hare provides the perfect model.

AN EXAMPLE: THE LYNX-HARE RELATIONSHIP

Studies have shown that cyclic declines in snowshoe hare populations in Northern boreal forests are linked to excessive browsing during population increases, which creates a food shortage. The high mortality caused by nutritional deficiency reduces hare populations and, thus, impairs reproduction the following breeding season.

The hare is the primary food source of the Canada lynx, and a decline in hares causes a sharp drop in lynx numbers and a reduction in recruitment of young lynx into the population. Predator populations stabilize somewhat at lower levels until, with a decline of predators and a growing abundance of winter foods, hare populations rebound and the cycle is repeated.

The predators we hunt—coyotes, foxes, cats, raccoons and all else—live and die by similar codependencies. It is not necessary to understand the complexities of predator/prey relationships to be a good hunter. But it is key to explaining why hiding in a bush and imitating a predator's supper is an effective means of hunting them.

ADD MAN TO THE EQUATION

But there's another key variable to consider. It would be folly to exclude man, the hunter, from nature's equation for equilibrium, for we too can have a cyclic effect on the predators we hunt and, in turn, the prey species they hunt.

Generally, we do not hunt predators to eat them—or to sustain ourselves monetarily. However, the value of fur and the relative profitability of harvesting it have historically impacted how aggressively we hunt furbearing animals, and how we affect their populations.

In a study conducted by the American Sheep Industry Association, there was a positive correlation between the price paid for a coyote pelt and the number of coyotes harvested that year. Knowing this, it probably won't surprise you that this, in turn,

Predators learn at an early age that hearing distress screams from prey species means that a warm meal might be just minutes away.

reduced the rate of predation on domestic livestock and, no doubt, wild prey species.

Back in 1982, coyote pelts brought an average price of $34.92, and 421,000 coyotes were harvested by private fur hunters and trappers. However, a decade later, when the average price paid for coyote pelts had dropped to $13.53, the annual harvest decreased to 158,000. That's a 63 percent decrease in 10 years. Coyotes were still abundant, but it wasn't as profitable to hunt or trap them.

Studies show a correlation between the number of coyotes harvested and the number of sheep they kill. When fur prices are low and harvest is reduced, fewer coyotes are harvested and sheep depredation increases.

The Biology of Predator Hunting

In the late 1970s and early 1980s, prime mountain-type coyote pelts were extremely valuable, some bringing in as much as $100.

Sheep and lamb losses in states where annual data were available increased from 6.9 percent of the stock sheep and new-crop lamb inventory in 1983, to 11.7 percent of the same inventory in 1994, a 70 percent increase.

The repercussions of a diminished fur harvest effort were also felt in the Dakota prairie pothole regions, where predator numbers increased (red foxes, raccoons and skunks, primarily) and impaired ground-nesting bird recruitment.

An experiment conducted by the Delta Waterfowl Foundation, examining the effects of predation on ground-nesting birds, found that areas where predators were removed had an average of 70 percent apparent nest success for upland nesting ducks. In adjacent locations, where no predator control was exercised, ducks only experienced 39 percent success.

Many wildlife biologists agree that predators are the number one factor limiting duck population growth. Those biologists would probably also agree that fur hunters and trappers are the primary agents of predator control. We directly affect waterfowl nesting success by choosing to harvest less fur when prices are down.

This creates a good news/bad news scenario for avid predator hunters. The bad news first.

BAD NEWS, GOOD NEWS

Since fur prices crashed back in 1987, it has been less profitable to hunt and trap furbearing animals. Select mountain-type coyotes that were once worth $100, red foxes that fetched $80 and Western bobcats that demanded $500 are far less valuable in today's market. Changes in fashion, economic upheaval in foreign markets and (to a lesser extent) anti-fur campaigns waged by anti-trapping and anti-hunting groups, have all combined to make fur harvesting less profitable. Consequently, less fur is being harvested than when prices were more favorable; predator populations are on the rise.

As predator populations grow, they have an adverse effect on game and nongame species, as well as domestic stock. The presence of mange, parvo, distemper and other diseases is becoming more prevalent as predator populations in some areas reach and exceed the carrying capacity of their habitats. Death by disease is often nature's answer to overpopulation.

The good news? We can help, by choosing to harvest more predators even though profitability is diminished. There has never been a better time to dust off the varmint rifle and round up your favorite calls and camo. It's the perfect opportunity to initiate a new domino effect—one that will reduce predator numbers and produce a more vibrant animal community; one that will extend your time in the field deep into the winter months and keep you out in the field hunting when you thought hunting season was only a fleeting dream or something to wait for.

Predators such as coyotes, foxes, raccoons and skunks can have a detrimental effect on ground-nesting birds like waterfowl.

Lower fur prices have meant good news to some fur hunters. With fewer trappers in the field, predator populations are at all-time highs and hunting opportunities have never been better.

The Biology of Predator Hunting

DISTRESS SCREAMS & WHAT THEY MEAN TO PREDATORS

I distinctly remember the first time I picked up an injured rabbit. The shrill screams that followed (the rabbit's and then mine!) left a lasting impression. And without doubt, each young coyote, fox or bobcat that captures its first warm meal quickly makes the association between those screams and the protein they represent.

There are several theories on why prey species scream when in the clutches of a predator. The obvious pain and terror associated with being eaten alive immediately jump to mind, but there might be underlying, more altruistic or territorial reasons for this behavior. Or it might be a final strategy—one of surprise—for defense and escape.

TERROR

Gerry Blair, one of the all-time predator hunting greats, believes that prey animals, when they get a close-up look at the dental work of canines and felines or the equally dreaded beak and talon of flying raptors, articulate their terror as a response to the inevitable fact that they are about to be killed and eaten.

In the case of raptors, Gerry explains that, "The prey is located from aloft. The critter swoops, stoops or soars to the target, taking hold with its razor-sharp talons, which encircle the rabbit's ribcage. Death is by suffocation. The hunter holds tight and the rabbit screams, losing a bit of air. The talons tighten a bit further to compress the lungs. Scream. Tighten. The process might take a minute or more, substantially longer if the hold is not precise. During all of that time, as air allows, the rabbit screams piteously."

And that, Gerry says, is key to why other predators arrive on the scene.

"Other predators within hearing range hustle in to have a look, hoping to steal the meal," he says. "A hungry coyote, fox or bobcat has no conscience. Each is likely to kick a red-tailed hawk's butt bad and take away his lunch. A hawk that objects too much is likely to join the cottontail within the belly of the beast."

According to Gerry's explanation, the scream signals a dinner-bell response. If the predator is high on the food chain and its hunting style is that of a hard-charger, such as a coyote, the response will typically be immediate and aggressive. With little fear that an even larger predator will be at the other end of the scream, these animals have the luxury of confidence.

Red and gray foxes, and even bobcats, must exercise more caution when approaching what might turn out to be a larger predator on a kill. A careless fox, for instance, might end up as a coyote's dessert.

ALTRUISM

Altruism refers to the selfless concern for the welfare of others. Many people believe that animals scream to warn others of their kind that danger is at hand and to get away while the getting is good. This, they say, is a conditioned response that puts the good of the community above the well-being of the individual. Thus, this theory would suggest, the rabbit that has fallen victim to the hawk screams to warn other rabbits without concern about its own inevitable undoing.

But the bottom line is the same: To every predator within earshot, the screaming translates into an opportunity for a meal.

ESCAPE!

One explanation of the scream response holds that prey animals scream to attract other predators! While this notion might seem odd at first consideration, the reasoning behind this hypothesis provokes some thought.

University of Saskatchewan researchers conducted a series of experiments to analyze predator/prey relationships in fish. Minnows release chemical pheromones after being attacked and, just like the screams of a rabbit, those pheromones attract predators. The researchers hypothesized that an animal's chances of escape increased when a second predator approached and tried to steal the prey from the first

One theory as to why an animal screams when in the clutches of a predator is that it warns others of its kind to flee immediately because danger is in the area.

predator, and that the pheromones were a reactionary defense mechanism. Interestingly, experiments upheld this theory. The study showed that when minnows in the wild released chemical alarm substances they escaped from pike more often than minnows without alarm substances.

Could it be that a rabbit's scream is a conditioned response to attract other predators? No experiments have been conducted to support this theory, but it seems reasonable that there could be a correlation.

A NATURAL RESPONSE

For whatever reason prey animals scream when in the clutches of a predator, the result is predictable: Other predators respond.

And that, my friends, is why the biology of those conditioned responses is important to us. Because, you see, there are really three conditioned responses at work and they define the very nature of our sport. The rabbit is conditioned to scream when attacked by a predator. The predator is conditioned to respond to those screams in hopes of securing a meal. And you and I are conditioned to take advantage of this relationship—to hide in the bush pretending to be a coyote's supper in hopes of calling predators sure-kill close.

One study suggests that prey animals, such as this pheasant, use distress cries to attract other predators and cause competition that may provide an opportunity for escape.

The Biology of Predator Hunting

COMPETITION AMONG PREDATORS

Animal communities are based on mutually beneficial relationships that help maintain equilibrium between the flora and fauna in a complex environment. We've looked at the relationships between predators and prey species, but of equal interest and importance is the interaction and competition between like species.

Most of the predators that we hunt live within structured social families that are based on aggressiveness and intolerance—the dominance of individual animals over others. These hierarchies maintain order and structure and provide a mechanism that guards against interbreeding, disease, over-crowding and the devastation of available resources.

Dispersal (which occurs as young animals are pushed from their home ranges and seek out new territories) allows for population growth and distribution of the species as a whole.

There is also competition between different predatory species that vie for the same territories and their resources. Again, the most dominant species generally inhabit the most desirable and productive locales while subordinate species seek out habitat niches where they can avoid being attacked.

INTRASPECIFIC COMPETITION

Population regulation and territory acquisition involve competition for resources among members of the same species. Ecologists refer to this as intraspecific competition. This rivalry becomes vigorous when prime habitat is in short supply and food sources are scarce.

During many hunts in the high desert regions of Arizona, for instance, I have observed as many as four coyotes responding to a call at one time, often arriving from different directions. This type of fierce competition makes for exciting hunts and confirms the effectiveness of using food source sounds where predator populations are high and food is sparse.

Intraspecific competition leads to dispersal in predator populations. Instead of dealing with the stress of limited food sources and constant attacks from more dominant members of the society, young adult animals often flee and seek vacant habitat areas. These are often less desirable localities with fewer resources. Some predators perish from starvation or are killed by those animals whose territories they have trespassed upon.

As these animals gain maturity and dominance, many are able to migrate to better territories or occupy areas that have become vacant for whatever reason. Fur trappers know that they can set traps at the same locations year after year with continued success: As animals are removed from prime habitat, other animals will find these open, desirable niches and repopulate them.

Some coyotes cooperate by hunting in pairs.

In his book *Elements of Ecology*, Robert Leo Smith explains that more important to population regulation is dispersal that takes place when the population density is low or increasing, but well before the population reaches a density at which food and cover are overexploited.

"Individuals who participate are not a random selection of the population but ones that are in good condition, belong to any sex or age group, have a good chance of survival, and show a high probability of settling in a new area. Some evidence exists that such individuals are genetically predisposed to disperse.

"Such individuals can maximize their fitness only if they leave their birthplace. When intraspecific competition at the home place is intense, dispersers can locate in habitats where resources are more accessible, breeding sites are more available and competition is less. Further, the individual reduces the danger of inbreeding. At the same time, dispersers also incur risks. They are living in unfamiliar terrain; their hybrid young, produced with wholly

Intraspecific competition leads to the dispersal of sub-adults. Rather than deal with the stress of limited food sources and constant attacks from more dominant members of the society, they venture off on their own in search of vacant habitat niches.

The Biology of Predator Hunting

unrelated individuals, may not be well adapted to the environment."

Dispersal is a function of population density control and population expansion. A good example is provided by the relatively recent movement of coyotes into the eastern reaches of the North American continent. And while this is a function of intraspecific competition and dispersal, it has also been a function of competition between different predatory species.

Historically, wolves kept coyote populations at bay where they coexisted, and coyotes were not found in abundance in the East. When man stepped in and removed wolves, this opened up new territories and paved the way for the coyote's eastward migration.

INTERSPECIFIC COMPETITION

Interspecific competition concerns the competition for resources among different species. The classic relationship between coyotes and red foxes in North Dakota provides a good example. These predators compete vigorously for the same limited food sources contained in optimal habitat niches.

The coyote occupies a higher position on the food chain and considers the red fox unwanted competition. Coyotes will run off or kill the smaller predators that infringe on their territories. But foxes must survive under the constant threat posed by the larger predator and, essentially, find niches in the habitat that coyotes find less desirable.

"It's not a friendly relationship, let's put it that way," describes Steve Allen, retired furbearer biologist for the North Dakota Wildlife Division. Allen, an avid predator hunter, participated in a number of studies that observed the relationships between red foxes and coyotes in North Dakota. He says that the results are interesting from a hunter's perspective as well as from that of a biologist.

"It's the same with all the canines. Each species likes its own kind, but everybody hates the other guy," Steve says. "And that particularly holds true in the case of coyotes and red foxes. Coyotes drive red foxes from their territories, often killing them. Smart foxes figure this out and go where there aren't any coyotes. That's how coyotes end up in some areas and foxes end up in others."

A study published in 1987 looked at the relationships between these two predators and came up with some interesting findings regarding how the animals utilize the North Dakota landscape. It was found that coyotes center their activities, especially pup rearing, on relatively large roadless areas where cropland is least abundant. Foxes live closer to farmsteads and roads where cropland is most abundant.

The study concluded that coyotes and red foxes tended to avoid interspecific encounters. This

Competition for food sources between predatory species can be intense. Coyotes will run off or kill smaller predators like foxes.

explained the absence of red foxes from much of the area where there was little cropland, the areas where coyotes were most abundant.

This relationship holds true where coyotes and gray foxes share the same habitat. For example, in Texas, gray fox are generally less abundant where coyotes are common. However, on ranches where coyotes have been removed by trappers and hunters because of the threat they pose to sheep and other grazing livestock, gray fox are plentiful. It appears that coyotes hold gray foxes numbers in check where the two species occupy the same territory.

Dominant animals vigorously defend their territories from intruders.

TERRITORIALITY

All predators stake out territories and vigorously defend them from poachers. Territoriality is one mechanism whereby the population density of a species is adjusted to the availability of resources such as food and water. Each territory holder is defending itself and its family. When all the critical resources (i.e., food) have been divided between territories, any remaining animals face little more than the prospect of starvation (or at least not breeding) until they can establish a territory that becomes vacant.

In the North Dakota study, it was found that coyotes and red foxes avoided contact with each other. Foxes avoided coyotes, which caused foxes to shy away from occupying central portions of coyote family territories and to limit their use of areas within coyote territory. To frequent coyote territory could cause conflict, which could result in the deaths of foxes.

The study also found that age and social status might be important factors affecting relationships between individual coyotes and foxes. Young foxes are probably most vulnerable to mortality from coyotes, especially when dispersing, because they are inexperienced and travel through unfamiliar terrain, including coyote territories.

Smith points out that the degree of aggressive behavior among individuals might limit the size of their home range. Dominant males can control highly desirable locations, especially in relation to food and females, and force subdominant animals to occupy the areas that are left. Restriction to a home area also confers security. Animals become familiar with the location of food, shelter and escape cover.

All predators stake out territories and defend them from poachers, even poachers of the same species.

The Biology of Predator Hunting

VOCALIZATIONS & SOCIALIZATIONS

While hunting turkeys in the Missouri Breaks of South Dakota a few years ago, I was enjoying a long hike back to my truck after a successful morning hunt, 12 gauge slung over one shoulder and a handsome Merriam's longbeard over the other. Lost in pleasant thoughts, I nearly missed the young coyote that was busily mousing on a grassy hill about a quarter mile away. I ducked behind some scant cover and watched the inexperienced youngster hunt for breakfast.

Cupping my hand to my mouth, I barked out a challenge, mustering my most threatening "big dog on the block" voice. The reaction I got surprised and amused me. The poor pup flattened to the ground and lay motionless, trying to become one with the prairie duff. He never twitched a muscle in the 15 minutes that I watched him. I suspect that this young dog had been the victim of a severe beating or two at the hand of a more dominate male coyote and was hoping to avoid a rematch.

Before sunrise the next morning, I was back at that same location, hoping to pick a fight. I settled in and waited for the first inklings of dawn. Once I could make out my surroundings, I lifted my howler to my mouth and delivered the most menacing barks and short, choppy howls in my repertoire—the kind big dogs are made of. Seconds later, a large coyote broke the horizon better than a quarter mile away, making a beeline toward me at full throttle.

The coyote gained momentum on the downhill slope, crossed the creekbottom without breaking stride and then powered up the hill that separated us, closing the precious ground between us at an alarming

Extremely social and expressive animals, coyotes communicate territoriality, social status, and parenting and mating cues, through a mixture of vocalizations.

rate. Uncomfortable with the vanishing real estate that separated us, I barked out a loud warning. The coyote skidded to a halt, hackles at full mast. A 70-grain ballistic-tip bullet ended the drama.

That event left a strong impression regarding the intense territorial nature of these animals. It also gave me the confidence to use vocalizations—not only to locate coyotes but to call them in.

BREAKING THE RULES

Too many callers, I think, are firmly stuck in a rabbit-in-distress-call rut. Maybe this approach has produced somewhat consistent results. Or maybe the hunter knows very little about howling and coyote behavior or is just reluctant to try something new. Unfortunately, these hunters are severely limiting their potential for success.

Scott Huber, an animal damage control agent for the South Dakota Division of Wildlife, says that hunters can utilize howling to sell a coyote or group of coyotes on the idea that there's another coyote in the area. And if you use howling in addition to rabbit wailings, he says, it gives them added confidence when they're coming in to a call. The howl also provides more volume and distance than you get with a rabbit call.

"I think that younger coyotes come to howling for social reasons whereas older coyotes probably come more for territorial reasons," he says. "A lot of times they'll answer you and you can set up accordingly."

"A rule of thumb is that if they're close, they'll come in without answering … they'll just show up," Scott explains. "If they are medium range, they'll sometimes answer you and then come in. And if they're a long way off and they don't really feel like coming, they'll answer and keep answering. Generally, in that situation, you've got to move toward them."

The Biology of Predator Hunting

Imitating the vocalizations coyotes use to communicate is an effective means of locating and calling them in.

UNDERSTAND THE ANIMAL

The more you know about coyotes, the more successful you're going to be. And the best callers I've shared company with have been those who understand a great deal about the animals they hunt. Huber says that coyotes are constantly changing their habits because of hunting pressure or changes in their environment or food sources. The hunter has to read those changes and adjust his hunting style.

While coyotes are the most vocal of the predators we hunt (and when we talk about using vocalizations to call predators, we are generally talking about coyotes), foxes and even bobcats communicate vocally as well, albeit on a more subtle basis. There are sounds you can use on foxes and bobcats,

however, that are effective when food-source sounds are not working. These include the distress cries of their young and fighting sounds.

Using the actual sounds of young canines in distress or canines fighting will often entice both red and gray foxes to come in for a look. These territorial and curiosity responses are especially valuable when hunting in areas where hunters have educated predators to the typical rabbit screams.

So don't limit your success by becoming singular in your approach to calling coyotes or other predators. If you're stuck in the rabbit-in-distress rut, you are only utilizing one aspect of a predator's tendency to respond to the call. You have effectively tied one hand behind your back.

Talking to Coyotes

Most animals communicate, to one degree or another, through the use of body language and/or vocalizations. Coyotes, in particular, are extremely social and expressive animals. They communicate territoriality, social status and parenting and mating cues through a mixture of body language, howls, whines, growls and barks.

The late Bill Austin, one of the all-time predator hunting greats, was a master of coyote behavior. He identified a number of coyote vocalizations and was one of the pioneers of using these sounds to call and hunt coyotes. The following are some basic sounds that he identified, and their possible applications.

Domain Call: Coyotes are extremely territorial and the domain call declares dominance. It consists of a lot of aggressive barking and short squalls and should only be used when attempting to call in other adult males. This call is likely to scare off pre-adult dogs.

Female Invitation: This is a friendly call and is more likely to get a response from young, nonaggressive coyotes in the fall. Typically, these youngsters will howl to announce their presence and then come to a friendly howl. These are long, trailing, high-pitched howls of a nonaggressive nature.

Coyote Love Song: This is the sound of a pair of coyotes, male and female, howling together. This call can be produced by a pair of callers using friendly barks and howls. Males generally produce lower-pitched howls than females.

Sunrise Serenade: The Sunrise Serenade is an entire family group of coyotes howling together. There are cassette tapes on the market that produce this effect. This and the Coyote Love Song usually elicit howling from lone coyotes, or other groups of coyotes, and are good tools for locating coyotes.

By learning a few basic vocalizations, like barks and howls, you can increase your success in the field when coyotes don't respond to food-source sounds.

The Biology of Predator Hunting

Chapter Three

HUNTING EQUIPMENT

*F*rom an equipment standpoint, there has never been a better time to hunt predators. Special-purpose rifles and shotguns add a new dimension of form and function to our sport. Premium factory ammunition that rivals the accuracy of hand-turned loads is available to the average Joe, who might not have the time or inclination to reload cartridges or shotshells.

Camouflage clothing of every conceivable pattern and weight is quiet, and some is completely waterproof. Field-tough electronic tape, CD and digital-chip players with remote controls are available, and libraries of animal sounds are abundant. There are mouth calls of every conceivable design.

We have products for masking and eliminating human scent to fool the noses of the animals we hunt. Handheld global positioning systems guide us to our setups and then back to our truck.

Manufacturers produce specialized scopes, with incredible light-gathering capabilities, designed to complement long-range varmint calibers. High-power spotting scopes and binoculars help us sort out the critters from the cover.

High-power spotlights, shooting lights, night optics and other specialized products provide the necessary accoutrements for those of us who like to hunt the night shift. Rangefinders, reloading components, high-tech backpacking equipment ... the list goes on and on.

All this "stuff" is what makes annual gift giving (or should I say "gift receiving") times around the avid predator hunters' homes truly glorious occasions.

These advances in the technology of varmint hunting, coupled with high predator populations in most regions of North America, make these the best of times for the avid caller. All of this adds up to more productivity in the field and yes, let's face it, more fun.

FUR GUNS & LOADS

ince Buck turned the worn rifle trigger over and over in his fingers, alternating his unlit pipe from mouth to hand as he often does. Among his many hobbies, my father-in-law is an accomplished gunsmith. His patience for working with the inner mechanics of firearms has always astounded me, just as I'm sure my impatience annoys him on occasion.

"How many guns do you own, Vince?" I asked by way of making conversation.

"Oh, about 30, I guess," he answered without looking up.

"How many *varmint* guns?" I pressed, hoping to engage him in my favorite topic.

Looking up over his eyeglasses, he dead-panned the answer that held as much truth as humor. "About 30," he said, holding the trigger up to the light to have a better look.

While it is true that most rifle calibers from the mighty-mouse .22 rimfires to the menacing magnums will put an end to the predatory ways of lions, coyotes, foxes, bobcats, raccoons and all else, if you hope to preserve any dignity or profit, a certain amount of refinement is necessary.

Today's rifle hunters are specialists, and this is especially true of varmint hunters. All have their favorite makes, models and calibers, and most will swear by this configuration or that. But the truth of the matter is that the quintessential predator gun does not exist. It is, at best, a figment of the varmint hunter's mind, a topic of countless hours of argument at local gun shops.

Old-school varminteers often had a favorite rifle chambered to do a decent job on big game while doing an equally decent job on the predators and varmints they hunted. A 20 or 12 gauge shotgun of utilitarian design usually provided decent enough firepower needed for small game, waterfowl and the occasional furred critter. The operative word here, of course, is decent. Often, the .243 Win., which did a marginally good job on big game, killed most varmints with more gusto than necessary. And long-barreled shotguns used in the waterfowl blind were often too cumbersome for predator hunting. Excessive fur damage and diminished efficiency afield translated into a smaller fur check, especially unfortunate when a high-country coyote fetched $100.

The quintessential predator gun does not exist, so most predator hunters own several: smaller calibers for small critters and larger bores for larger critters.

TRICK: KILL THE ANIMAL, PRESERVE THE PELT

Dedicated predator hunters recognize the need for specialized guns and ammunition that are accurate and do minimal fur damage to serve the dual purpose of effectively killing predators while preserving a dignified pelt for the fur buyer.

Some hunters have even gone as far as owning specialized calibers for the various predators and terrain they hunted. For example, a Western hunter might opt for a long-range caliber, say a .22-250 Rem., and loads that reflect the expansive nature of landscape they frequently hunt, while an Eastern hunter might be more concerned with calibers and loads more friendly to the populated nature of the East. Both might find value in a shotgun that can rug out a hard-charging coyote at 40 yards, or a rimfire that treats red and gray fox pelts with respect.

Rifles to fill every conceivable varmint hunting niche, along with specialized factory loads, are testament to a growing interest in predator hunting. Shotgun configurations and special-purpose loads have seen a transformation from general multipurpose to species-specific applications.

And don't forget the rimfires, which have also seen a recent resurgence. New offerings in rifle configurations and ammunition have brought back the popularity of these diminutive fur-getters. Those hunters who pursue red and gray foxes have taken a particular liking to this mild-mannered option when long-range shots or large predators are not likely.

GUN DECISIONS

What does all this mean? If you're a casual hunter, probably not a lot. You will likely get by with the same rifle/shotgun combination that your grandfather used to take a variety of big and small game, and you'll do a decent job of it. If you're a dyed-in-the-wool varminteer, you probably already own a battery of rifles and shotguns and have many more on your wish list. If you're somewhere in between, as most hunters are, you must face the realization that no one rifle, no one shotgun, no single load configuration is going to accommodate all types of hunting in all types of terrain, on all types of critters.

Vince was right in one respect: Most centerfire calibers, old or new, have the capacity to kill all the predators we hunt. It's up to you to take it to the next level, if you have the desire. Making sure that the animal does not run off wounded—and preserving a decent pelt for the fur buyer—should be paramount in every predator hunter's mind. Having the right tools to accomplish this is something we should all strive for.

Many predator hunters opt for the .22 Win. Mag. rimfire as their primary fox and raccoon rifle.

Hunting Equipment

CENTERFIRE RIFLES

The centerfire rifle is the mainstay of the varminteer's gun collection. Whether they hunt east or west of the big river, most predator hunters own one or more .22 caliber centerfire rifles, and perhaps several of a more specialized nature—maybe a .17 Rem., a nifty wildcat or two, or something with muscle enough to buck moderate wind, like a .25-06 Rem. or .243 Win.

The consummate varmint rifle has several distinguishing characteristics that set it apart from standard models. It is designed purely for function over form. There's rarely anything "pretty" about a varmint rifle, except maybe in the eye of the beholder.

A predator gun needs to be field-friendly, designed specifically for the purpose of getting the job done in the most efficient manner. It should be equipped only with those accessories that enhance practicability and productivity.

The first thing I do when I take a new predator gun out of the box is attach a shoulder sling. I do considerably more walking than shooting, and I also carry a lot of "junk" to the stand—a cushion to sit on, shooting sticks, optics, hand calls and sometimes an electronic caller. I want my rifle shouldered and out of the way.

Predators have keen eyes and are sensitive to any movement on the landscape. There is no place for fancy gloss finishes or shiny barrels or optics on a varmint rifle. Many guns arrive from the factory with flat black or camo finishes designed with the sniper in mind. Other options include camo'd gun sleeves, tape or paint. Stay away from stainless steel finishes unless you plan to tape them up or otherwise conceal their shiny nature.

Bipods or shooting sticks are standard-issue gear. Predators often hang up at considerable distances and, unless you're a much better off-hand shooter than I, you'll need a rock-solid rest to get the job done. Bipods are essential when you're lying in the prone position, as many hunters do in the open expanses of the Dakota prairies or Western plains.

Fur Loads

Ideally, a varmint bullet is designed to deliver stability for long-range flight and then do minimal fur damage when it reaches its target. But, of course, this requires trade-offs. Bullets that carry the velocity and energy needed to reach out and touch a coyote in the next ZIP code often treat fur with little respect.

There are two schools of thought in regard to what constitutes a good fur bullet. The first school says that the bullet should pass cleanly through the body cavity of the critter, leaving a small entrance wound and a slightly larger exit wound that can be easily repaired with needle and thread. Full-metal jackets fall into this category. The danger, though, is that these bullets are designed for

Bolt-action centerfire rifles are the varminteer's mainstay. These guns are designed for accuracy and dependability.

minimum expansion. And while they zip through the critter without causing much fur damage, animals run a considerable distance before they die, making retrieval much more difficult.

The second school of thought is that the bullet should be designed to enter the body cavity and explode without exiting, thus releasing all of its energy within the animal and leaving no exit wound. Hollow-point and plastic-tipped bullets fall into this category. Hollow points have long been a favorite among fur hunters, and plastic-tipped bullets have gained popularity in recent years because of their inherent accuracy and fur-friendly nature.

According to gun writer Bryce Towsley, the primary advantage of the plastic-tipped bullet is that it allows for a sharp profile and a very small meplat (the flat leading edge of a bullet), which results in a high ballistic coefficient—the highest of any hunting bullet design. He points out that the plastic nose is less likely to deform than a lead tip and this results in a very consistent ballistic coefficient from bullet to bullet.

A solid rest is paramount to success. Shooting sticks or bipods are standard predator-hunting equipment.

Another advantage with the plastic-tipped bullet is that its center of gravity is moved slightly back, creating better stability in flight, similar to the concept that allows the superior accuracy in hollow-point match bullets.

Always keep in mind, however, that bullet placement is the key to controlling fur damage. Any bullet design will damage fur if bullet placement is sloppy.

Top Dogs

There are probably as many philosophies regarding what makes a good fur caliber as there are varmint hunters. Selecting the right caliber or calibers for you will depend on personal preferences, the type of terrain you hunt, the animals you intend to hunt and many other factors.

The following are profiles of a few of the most popular varmint calibers. See the sidebar "Point-Blank Sighting-In" (page 41) for an explanation of Maximum Point-Blank Range (MPBR) and how to utilize it.

Maximum Point-Blank Range (MPBR)

Caliber	Velocity (feet per second)	Bullet Weight (grains)	MPBR @ 200 yds. (in yards)
.17 Rem.	3,800	25	276.2
.22 Hornet	2,700	45	208.0
.223 Rem.	3,300	50	254.6
.222 Rem. Mag.	3,400	45	237.2
.22-250 Rem.	3,600	52	274.3
.243 Win.	3,400	70	270.0

Maximum Point-Blank Range (MPBR) is the distance out to which you can hold your crosshairs or sights on target and achieve a hit, depending on how you are sighted in. Most of the calibers favored by serious predator hunters are capable of producing high velocities, which translates into generous foot-pounds of energy downrange and flat trajectory to considerable ranges.

.17 Remington

This caliber has gained popularity in recent years, especially among Eastern hunters. Its light recoil and dainty bullet make it a favorite among red and gray fox hunters. Although this caliber is capable of reaching out with considerable consistency to 300 yards and beyond, it should be considered a medium-range caliber because of its inability to buck the wind. The .17 Rem. is an excellent varmint and small game cartridge in settled areas because of its mild report and inherent accuracy.

.22 Hornet

Another of the mighty-mouse calibers, the .22 Hornet was one of the first high-velocity, flat-trajectory varmint calibers produced. Developed in the 1920s by Captain G.L. Wotkyns, Townsend Whelen and several others at Springfield Armory, this caliber has experienced ebbs and flows in popularity. Savage produced the first factory rifle to chamber this round in 1932 and was closely followed by Winchester in 1933. The .22 Hornet has experienced some renewed interest in recent years, thanks in part

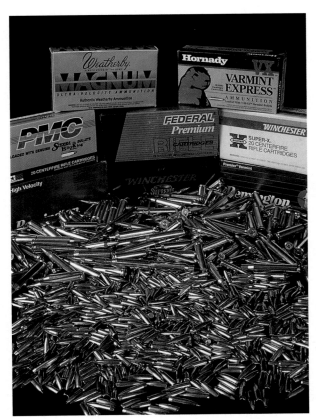

Today's predator hunter can choose from a wide array of ammunition specially designed for the sport.

to Ruger for chambering the round in its No. 3 carbine and Model 77/22 rifles, and to Thompson Center for chambering it in their Contender pistol.

.223 Remington

The .223 Rem. is popular among fur hunters because of its accuracy, flat trajectory and mild recoil. Capable of dealing with the toughest coyotes, it is most popular with fox hunters in the East, where the .22-250 Rem. and other similar calibers provide more muscle than is often needed. Originally developed as a military round in the late 1950s, it was later introduced by Remington as a commercial round. The .223 Rem. is a favorite with reloaders because of the availability of once-fired military brass.

.222 Remington Magnum

Also intended for military use, this cartridge was introduced for sporting use in 1958. While the .222 Rem. Mag. was not able to achieve the instant popularity of the .222 Rem., its expanded powder capacity and resulting increased velocity and energy made it a superior long-range round. It handles heavier bullets than the .222 Rem. can, making it slightly superior when shooting in wind or at long ranges.

.22-250 Remington

A necked-down version of the 250-3000, the .22-250 Rem. was introduced as a wildcat caliber more than 50 years ago. In 1967, Remington began production of this cartridge in its Model 700 series rifle. This has become the most popular of the fur calibers ever developed and is particularly favored by Western hunters because of its legitimate 300-yard-plus capabilities. Often dubbed the "Varminteer," the .22-250 Rem. has a reputation for accuracy and high velocity.

.243 Winchester

In 1955, Winchester necked down its .308 to 6mm, resulting in the .243 Win. The availability of a wide variety of bullet weights and designs makes this caliber a good choice for everything from prairie dogs to deer. As a fur gun, the .243 Win. can be harsh at times, but with lighter bullets, this caliber can do a dandy job on coyotes if bullet placement is precise. It delivers more recoil than the .22 center-fires but bucks the wind with greater proficiency, making it a good choice in the wide-open expanses of the West.

If I've missed your favorite caliber, take a number … and also take heart in the fact that we have so many great selections that it's impossible to mention them all here. Predator hunting is truly a species-specific activity and requires more than any one firearm can deliver. The presence of so many good fur calibers on the market is testament to the popularity of our sport.

Point-Blank Sighting-In

Because of the comprehensive nature of predator hunting, and the many circumstances hunters might find themselves in, many riflemen approach long-range accuracy using the point-blank method of sighting-in.

Predator-hunting action is often fast and furious, and hunters must make snap decisions regarding elevation and windage. These conditions require a rifle that shoots "flat" out to a calculated range. Thus, when point-blank sighting, you adjust the sights so that the trajectory of the bullet will not rise above or fall below predetermined range parameters.

In his NAHC book *Making Shots—A Rifle Hunter's Guide*, Bryce Towsley explains that point-blank sighting-in takes the guesswork out of determining where to hold on your target. "It helps to envision this as shooting through a pipe," Towsley writes. "The line of sight is exactly down the center of that pipe, and the sights are adjusted so that the bullet's path will never rise higher than the top of the pipe or fall below the bottom edge of the pipe until it reaches the maximum point-blank range."

A coyote's effective "kill zone" is approximately 4 inches. That is to say, if a coyote were standing broadside and you held dead-center on its vitals, your margin of error would

Spending time on the rifle range to get to know your firearms and how they perform at various distances gives you confidence when the time comes to pull the trigger on a coyote or fox standing 200 or more yards away.

be plus or minus 2 inches up or down for you to make an effective kill.

Let's look at a couple of examples of point-blank sighting using two popular fur calibers.

A .22-250 Rem. pushing a 53-grain Hornady HP Match bullet at 3,600 fps, sighted in at 200 yards, has a maximum point-blank range of 272.0 yards. That means that the bullet never rises more than 2 inches above or below "zero" between 0 and 272.0 yards. Using this sight-in, the bullet will zero at 235.4 yards. (At 300 yards, this bullet will be slightly more than 4 inches low.)

A .223 Rem. pushing a Hornady 45-grain Hornet bullet at 3,400 fps, sighted in at 200 yards, has a maximum point-blank range of 255.2 yards. This bullet "zeros" at 221.03 yards. (At 300 yards, this bullet will be about 6 inches low.)

Keep in mind that these calculations do not allow for wind velocity. Both bullets would be affected by wind velocity, and the lighter bullet would be more greatly affected.

Information on point-blank sighting and formulas for your favorite calibers and loads can be obtained from most ammunition manufacturers or reloading manuals. There are also several computer software programs available that will help you calculate point-blank ranges quickly and easily.

Most hunters grew up shooting .22 rimfires. Their light recoil and inexpensive ammunition make them a perfect fit for young shooters.

Rimfire Rifles

Many of us grew up tipping over pop cans and punching holes in paper with a .22 rimfire rifle of some sort.

Sensible parents recognize this diminutive caliber as a good choice for introducing their sons and daughters to the use of firearms: Ammunition is cheap, recoil is absent and a child can develop marksman skills and safety discipline before moving up to larger, more potent calibers.

The **.22 Long Rifle (.22 LR)** was introduced in the late 1800s and is easily the most popular cartridge in America today, with an estimated 2-billion-plus rounds discharged each year. Firearm manufacturers all offer rifles and handguns in this configuration and market them to paper-punchers and small game hunters alike. Major ammunition manufacturers offer an array of bullet designs for target shooting and hunting.

But while the .22 LR provides a good starting point for young marksmen, and is a favorite for target shooting and small game hunting, it lacks the knockdown power needed to anchor even medium-sized predators (such as foxes and bobcats) with consistency, let alone larger predators such as coyotes.

Winchester's introduction of the **.22 Win. Mag.** in 1959 provided a legitimate predator caliber in a rimfire casing. This muscled-up version of the .22 LR, combined with proper bullet configurations and proper bullet placement, does a decent job on close-quarter foxes and bobcats out to about 75 yards. The .22 Win. Mag., however, should not be considered when hunting coyotes or other more sturdy game.

A .22 Win. Mag. pushing a 40-grain hollow-point bullet delivers 133 more foot-pounds of energy and an additional 270 fps of velocity than a hyper-velocity .22 LR load with a lighter, 32-grain bullet. This translates into the extra energy needed to reach its target with enough power to penetrate and expand.

Hunters in the East, who must hunt in close proximity to human development, consider the .22 Win. Mag. a nifty option to centerfire calibers. Its mild report and diminished range is a good choice when

All major ammunition manufacturers offer .22 Long Rifle and .22 Win. Mag. ammo in an array of bullet designs for target shooting and hunting.

calling raccoons and foxes in small woodlots and around farm fields and timber edges. Western hunters, too, value this caliber if they are likely to encounter gray foxes and bobcats in the brushy ravines and rimrock where coyotes seldom venture. And you don't get the fur damage that you might with .22 centerfire cartridges.

Sighted in 1 inch high at 50 yards, the .22 Win. Mag. has a legitimate range of 100 yards. However, its energy drops significantly past 100 yards, and this small bullet can be pushed off course by even the slightest wind. I generally limit my shots to 75 yards.

Rimfire Ammunition

Manufacturers have not overlooked the .22 Mag.'s potential as a legitimate varmint caliber, and in recent years have developed new and improved cartridge designs built for accuracy and lethal expansion.

Remington's .22 Win. Mag. Premier, which features a 33-grain Hornady V-Max boattail bullet, is a good example. This bullet design offers excellent accuracy, rapid expansion and maximum terminal performance needed for extended-range shooting. Winchester's .22 Win. Mag. utilizes a jacketed hollow-point 40-grain bullet that, with muzzle velocities of 1,910 fps and rapid expansion for effective kills, is a true performer on small- and medium-sized predators.

Winchester turns out two jacketed hollow points—with 40-grain and 34-grain bullets—and a full-metal jacket (FMJ) 40-grainer. The 34-grain FMJ is a screamer, with a muzzle velocity of 2,120 fps and 338 foot-pounds of energy at the muzzle.

The Federal Cartridge Company also offers magnum rimfire cartridges. Federal's Sierra jacketed hollow-point bullet provides the flat trajectory and controlled expansion needed for effectively killing predators. This 30-grain bullet leaves the barrel at 2,200 fps with a muzzle velocity of 325 foot-pounds. If zeroed at 50 yards, this bullet drops only 1½ inches by 100 yards.

The .22 Win. Mag. is a legitimate fur gun, provided you limit your shots to 75 yards or so and don't expect to buck heavy wind or to dispatch a larger animal like a coyote with any consistency. But if you do your part in regard to bullet placement, a .22 Win. Mag. will do its part in anchoring medium-sized predators such as foxes, bobcats and raccoons.

The .22 Win. Mag. does a decent job on medium-sized predators (such as red and gray foxes) out to about 75 yards.

Hunting Equipment

SHOTGUNS FOR PREDATOR HUNTERS

No serious predator caller leaves home without a special-purpose shotgun for up-close-and-personal work. And thanks to a boom in the popularity of turkey hunting in recent years, there is no shortage of scatterguns that precisely fit the predator-hunting profile. Shotguns with interchangeable chokes, short barrels and camouflage or flat-black finishes serve the predator hunter well.

Many uninitiated predator hunters are reluctant to use shotguns, questioning the weapons' knockdown ability. The hunters have convinced themselves that even at close range, a rifle is the predator hunter's best friend. But at close range, shotguns,

with the proper loads and the right chokes, provide plenty of knockdown power and give the hunter more margin for error.

By way of comparison, one double-ought shotshell pellet is basically equivalent to a low-velocity .38 caliber handgun projectile. A 00 load contains nine pellets and in a tightly choked barrel spreads to about a 15-inch pattern at 20 yards. At close range the energy of the pellets acts as one mass, which, in this example, would be a velocity of 1,300 fps and kinetic energy of 2,100 foot-pounds. That's a lot of energy—and there's plenty left at 40 yards to effectively plant any predator.

The reason larger shot has more knockdown ability at longer ranges is that energy is divided between the pellets. Fewer, larger pellets carry more energy.

And in case you're wondering, shotguns are fur-friendly; most fur buyers don't even give the small holes in the pelt a second thought.

Best Loads

Since there is considerable difference between a 35- to 45-pound coyote and an 8-pound red or 10-pound gray fox, it is reasonable to assume that some loads will perform better for specific species than others in relation to knockdown ability and fur damage. So let's look at what might be considered optimal loads for five of the predators we hunt.

Coyotes

Coyotes are tough animals and body size can vary from a 25-pound average in the Southwest to 40-pounds-plus in the Northeast. Forget about the No. 4s or No. 6s that you might use to tame a fox or bobcat. These dogs require serious knockdown power! And shotguns, when loaded properly, will do the job with gusto. I have seen Gerry Blair rug out desert coyotes (which run on the smaller side) out to 50 yards and beyond with his Ithaca 10 gauge loaded with copper-plated BBs. No. 4 buckshot gets my nod as an all-around load for coyotes.

Experiment with different choke constrictions and don't assume that tighter will always be better, especially when you're shooting buckshot.

With hefty loads and the right chokes, shotguns provide plenty of knockdown power out to about 40 yards.

No. 4 or No. 6 shot in a 3-inch 12 gauge shell might be lethal on foxes, raccoons and bobcats, but you'll need to step up to buckshot or BBs to consistently anchor coyotes.

Red Foxes

Take away the red fox's dense coat and long, bushy tail, and you're looking at a critter about the size of an ordinary house cat. Needless to say, this animal will take a lot less abuse than a coyote if you want to preserve its beautiful fur.

No. 6 shot in a tightly choked 12 gauge is a good choice for this small predator. You should easily have an effective range to 35 yards, and might be able to stretch that a bit if you're shooting one of the 3-inch twelves especially developed for turkey hunting.

Gray Foxes

The gray fox is somewhat stockier than its red cousin but still doesn't require the hefty loads you would use for coyotes. No. 6s or No. 4s do a dandy job on this aggressive little critter. Again, a tight choke in a short-barreled gun is the ticket for fast, close action.

Bobcats

A bobcat can weigh in excess of 35 pounds but is not nearly as stout as a coyote. Go for the close shot and use shotshells that are fur-friendly. Even in today's flat fur market, a prime Western bobcat pelt can bring as much as $150.

Raccoons

The masked bandit is generally small of body, and fur damage can be kept to a minimum by using light shotgun loads. Raccoons are mostly hunted at night, and shots are almost always within 30 yards. No. 6s should provide plenty of power yet leave a respectable pelt for the fur buyer.

While they are larger than foxes and raccoons, bobcats are not nearly as sturdy as coyotes. No. 4 shot will effectively deal with bobcats and preserve their valuable fur.

OPTICS FOR VARMINT HUNTING

I distinctly remember the exact moment when the concept of good optics hit home.

I was turkey hunting with Glen Lehman in South Dakota, watching a band of Merriam's turkeys meander along a hillside a good half mile away. Trying to

Hunting Equipment

The combination of a scoped rifle on a steady rest poses a deadly threat to all predators.

that sits on top of your favorite fur gun, you should never overlook or take for granted the value of good optics.

Rifle Scopes

A wise hunter once told me, "Buy the best glass you can afford. You can't hit what you can't see." Those words emphasize the need to top your best predator guns with optics that will allow you to get optimal performance. It doesn't make much sense to invest a bunch of money in a predator gun capable of punching minute-of-angle groups and then put substandard glass on it that inhibits that capability.

There are a number of factors to consider when purchasing a scope: the type of firearm on which it will sit, the animals you will be hunting, and the type of terrain in which you will be hunting.

Variable-power scopes have long been popular with those hunters who ask their guns to perform on a variety of animals under a lot of different conditions. Hunters who require their guns to do double duty on white-tailed deer and coyotes might opt for scopes that power down for quick work or for when high magnification is not necessary, and power up for a long-distance coyote or for when they're trying to judge the quality of a white-tailed buck's rack.

Early variable-power scopes were less refined than those on the market today. A rifle's zero would often shift as the hunter changed magnification. This

confirm the sex of the bird that was hanging to the back of the band in typical tom turkey fashion, I strained my eyes through a weak pair of budget binoculars. I turned to Glen, who was steadying his Zeiss 10X40s on his knees, and ventured a guess. "I think the one to the rear is a gobbler," I said uncertainly. "I'm pretty sure I can make out a beard."

"There are two toms," Glen returned without hesitation. "Looks like the bigger one has about inch-and-a-quarter spurs."

Whether it's binoculars, spotting scopes or the glass

High-quality binoculars and scopes pay huge dividends in the field, especially in poor light conditions.

problem has been alleviated in modern scopes.

If I'm hunting predators with a variable-power scope, I generally keep it at its lowest setting. That way, I'm best prepared for critters that show up at close range unannounced. And the way I figure it, I'll have plenty of time to crank it up for those paranoids that hold up and give me the bad-eye from several hundred yards out.

Many hunters prefer a fixed-power scope for its consistency. They say it's easier to judge the distance of animals if you're used to always seeing them at the same magnification when you look through your scope. Fixed-power scopes in the 4X to 8X range are most popular with predator hunters.

A scope's clarity and light-gathering capabilities are paramount. The size of the objective lens and the quality of the glass will determine the brightness of the image when you look through the scope. A 50mm objective lens, for example, has the capability of drawing in more light to your eye than a 32mm lens. This translates to better visibility, especially under low-light situations. As far as quality, you pay for what you get. Good glass translates into hard cash.

Most modern scopes from major manufacturers such as Zeiss, Leupold, Swarovski, Nikon, Bausch & Lomb and many others, feature multi-glass surfaces that transmit 90 percent or more of the available light to your eye. This provides a crisp, distortion-free image. Glass that is sealed and nitrogen-purged is rugged, waterproof and won't fog up.

Binoculars

Binoculars can be the predator hunter's best friend. A good hunting buddy, John Graham, an Animal Damage Control (ADC) trapper and predator hunter from Jordan, Montana, always uses binoculars to study the landscape during and after a calling session. He does so because he knows that suspicious critters often hold up at distances that make them difficult to discern with the naked eye. Spotting these paranoids might inspire him to sit a while longer and try to coax them in.

Field binoculars should be lightweight and durable, with high-quality glass. I generally like those that offer about 8X magnification because they are easy to hold steady and offer sufficient magnification for most field situations.

Even more important than the power, though, is the quality and light-gathering capability of the glass. This is usually the result of larger objective lenses that allow more light to the eyes. Glass quality is generally correlated to how much binoculars cost. Expect to spend several hundred dollars for high-quality binoculars.

Spotting scopes can be useful when scrutinizing the landscape at great distances for specks of fur.

Spotting Scopes

Spotting scopes are useful in the wide-open expanses of the West where property is measured in sections rather than acres. Most mount to the window of a pickup or on a tripod and can be used to scrutinize every nook and cranny in the landscape for specks of fur. Some hunters even carry spotting scopes along to the stand, using them to examine every blemish in the terrain before, during and after the setup. A straight 20-power scope is just right for the predator hunting job.

Take the advice of the wise hunter: Don't short-change yourself by trying to save a few bucks when purchasing optics. Investing the extra money in the glass you carry into the field will pay huge dividends each fur season.

Hunting Equipment

PREDATOR CALLS

Predator calls come in a variety of shapes and sizes in both open-reed and closed-reed configurations. They are relatively inexpensive and while various models are similar in construction, each call produces a somewhat unique and distinctive sound. That's why most serious predator hunters own several.

The assortment of predator calls on the market today is mind-boggling, as are the reasons for choosing a particular make and model. There are calls of open-reed and closed-reed configurations, of all shapes and sizes, made from every wood imaginable, as well as those turned from plastics, metals and other man-made materials. Many are as aesthetically pleasing to the eye as they are functional in the field.

There are large, boisterous calls designed to produce the substantial volume needed for long-distance calling in open terrain, or for those times when heavy winds, heavy vegetation or breaks in the landscape limit a smaller call's ability to reach the eager ears of hungry predators.

Other calls are specifically fashioned to produce the subtle squeaks of rodents and small birds for close-in work on nervous predators such as the red fox, or to entice those predators that are hung up just out of sight or out of gun range.

Some calls imitate the sounds of specific prey species, such as those that produce the piteous wailings of jackrabbits, snowshoe hares, cottontailed rabbits, squealing birds and rodents in distress. And there are calls finely tuned for species-specific calling, calculating prey sounds and volume desirable for particular predators.

Howlers created to produce the wide range of coyote vocalizations add another dimension to calling. Those hunters who are initiated in the social aspects of coyote behavior and their inherent social and territorial tendencies, gain another tool for fooling these crafty and often paranoid predators. Other hunters simply utilize howlers as a means of locating their quarry before descending on them armed with more traditional food-based calls to finish the job.

A growing number of hunters are adding electronic callers to their calling arsenals. These callers use cassette, digital and compact disc technology, and a wide array of recorded animal sounds. The mere availability of this new technology is a testament to the increased popularity of the sport. Electronics give the novice caller the confidence to go afield knowing full well that if his hunting skills are adequate, his lack of calling prowess won't hamper his success. And veterans know that recorded animal sounds give them a needed edge in hard-hunted areas where predators are highly educated and extremely suspicious.

SORTING THROUGH THE CALLS

In truth, most of the sounds produced by the above-mentioned calls will attract predators. Personal preference or hunting style usually dictates which types of calls the hunter carries to the field.

I use both electronic callers and hand calls and believe that there are times when one is more appropriate than the other. I often hike deep into the outback and do not like the extra weight and bulk associated with using electronics.

Hand calls are obviously less expensive than electronics, and you can own an entire collection of hand calls and howlers for the price of one electronic caller. And when used by experienced callers, hand calls are versatile and capable of producing a wide variety of sounds.

But having said that, I'll add that I've hunted areas where the added option of

Predator calls, both mouth-blown and electronic, appeal to all predators looking for a free meal.

using a wide variety of taped animal sounds, including many territorial sounds that you are unable to produce with hand calls, has provided the tools needed to turn a challenging day around.

The bottom line is that the predator hunter needs to remain versatile, which often means using a variety of tools to get the most of each situation. While you might have a preference for a certain type of call—and, if you're like me, you have favorites that you simply can't venture afield without—don't limit yourself by getting into a rut. By utilizing a variety of tools and by recognizing when one might give you an advantage over another, you will be better equipped to make a good day of calling better.

Let's take an in-depth look at the various calls used to call predators. We will explore each call's attributes and weaknesses, and discuss how to use each call effectively.

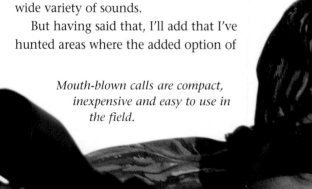

Mouth-blown calls are compact, inexpensive and easy to use in the field.

OPEN-REED CALLS

Open-reed calls are constructed utilizing a thin piece of mylar or plastic (the reed) that is fitted into a plastic, wooden or metal tube so that the reed is

Open-reed calls can produce a variety of animal sounds ranging from soft, coaxing rodent squeals to loud rabbit squalls, coyote barks, and puppy yips and cries.

Open-Reed Calls

Advantages

Open-reed calls add versatility in the hands of an experienced caller. They are capable of producing a wide range of sounds, and their volume is easy to control. In extremely cold weather, they perform better than closed-reed calls, because the exposed reed can be kept in the caller's mouth where it will not readily freeze as is often the case with closed-reed calls. Another advantage—no two callers sound alike on even the same model of open-reed call, because each caller holds a call in his mouth and positions his hands on the end of the tube differently. Educated predators are less likely to become call-shy in areas that see a lot of hunting pressure; if every hunter in the county were blowing the same closed-reed calls and producing nearly identical sounds on them, the predators would quickly learn to avoid that noise.

Disadvantages

The biggest disadvantage with open-reed calls is that they can be difficult to master. But with practice, any caller can become proficient on them. Another challenge: The exposed plastic reed is susceptible to heat damage and must never be left on the dash of your truck. Plastic reeds lose tonal quality with age and should be periodically replaced. Any slight damage to the reed will affect sound quality. It's a good idea to always keep an extra reed handy.

When to Use Open-Reed Calls

One of the reasons I often opt for an open-reed call is that I am able to produce a variety of sounds that I'm not able to get from a closed-reed model.

If I am calling coyotes, for example, I might use an open-reed call to imitate a rabbit in distress. If I call in a double and kill one coyote, I can get back on the call and produce the whines and yips of a distressed coyote either to stop the fleeing mate or sometimes even call it back in. You don't have that kind of flexibility with a closed-reed call.

Open-reed calls also make effective howlers. You can use these calls to imitate the barks and howls used to locate and call in coyotes. In a North Dakota study on predator hunting, response rates by red foxes to closed-reed hand calls greatly exceeded that for open-reed calls; however, response rates by coyotes to open-reed calls exceed that for closed-reed calls. Interestingly, I have found the opposite to be true. For red foxes, I have had better success using the subtle rodent squeaks and squeals best produced on an open-reed call, and for coyotes, I have generally had better luck with closed-reed calls.

exposed. A few models use thin metal reeds, but these are more susceptible to freezing in cold weather.

Open-reed calls are capable of producing a wide array of sounds that range from soft, coaxing rodent squeals to loud rabbit squalls, coyote barks and howls, and puppy yips and cries. Inherently versatile, these calls are most popular with experienced predator hunters who have put in the time required to become proficient with them.

While open-reed calls can be more difficult to master than closed-reed calls, many callers agree that the sounds produced by open-reed calls are superior. There are a number of open-reed calls on the market including the Johnny Stewart PC-6, TallyHo, Ed Sceery Open-Reed Predator and Crit'R•Calls Magnum, to mention a few.

BLOWING AN OPEN-REED CALL

An open-reed call, as the name suggests, utilizes an exposed reed in a plastic, wooden or metal body.

Cup one or both hands over the bell of the call and place the end of the reed in your mouth.

To make soft, subtle rodent squeals, cover only the tip of the reed with your lips and blow while simultaneously opening and closing your hand(s) over the bell of the call.

To imitate the sound of a bird in distress or to make the whining sounds of a canine pup in distress, place your lips about halfway up the reed. Again use your hand(s) on the bell to vary the pitch. For canine pup sounds, vary the pitch of the call from a low note to higher ones to imitate the pitiful cries.

To get loud rabbit squalls from an open-reed call, place your lips over the majority of the reed to produce these lower-pitched cries. Open-reed calls are capable of producing decent volume if necessary.

Coyote barks and howls can also be made using open-reed calls or howlers utilizing an open reed and an enlarged bell. Vary the pitch of the howls by changing where you place your lips on the reed. The closer you get to the tip of the reed, the higher the pitch.

Blow for about 20 seconds and then sit quietly for a minute or so. If nothing shows up, repeat the sequence. Stand at each location for 15 to 20 minutes if you're hunting coyotes or foxes, 30 minutes or more if you're after bobcats.

*To use an open-reed call, follow these steps: **1)** Cup the body of the call in your hand with the exposed reed on top. You can control volume by opening and closing your hand over the end of the tube. **2)** For high-pitched sounds, like those made by rodents and birds, place your lips over the tip of the reed and blow. **3)** For lower-pitched sounds (such as a screaming rabbit or coyote howl) place your lips closer to where the reed meets the tube.*

Hunting Equipment

Closed-Reed Calls

Closed-reed calls consist of a metal reed fully contained within the body of a tube. The tubes are made from a variety of materials including many types of

Less experienced callers favor closed-reed calls, which are easier to use than open-reed calls.

Closed-Reed Calls

Advantages

Pure and simple, the closed-reed call is easier to use than the open-reed call. Even the uninitiated caller can get convincing and consistent sounds from these tubes. They are durable, and the reeds are not as susceptible to heat and dirt as are open-reed models. Closed-reed calls are relatively inexpensive and a hunter can carry several models and sizes to get a variety of sounds as each setup dictates. These calls, especially the larger models, are capable of producing considerable volume and are a good choice in windy conditions or when vegetation and breaks in the terrain limit the call's range.

Disadvantages

While closed-reed calls are easy to blow, they do not provide the variety of sounds you can get from open-reed calls. This often leads to animals becoming call-shy where hunting pressure is considerable. Closed reeds can also fail in cold weather. It's the nature of the metal reed to freeze at the most inopportune times and become inoperable. If you do experience freeze-up, blow through the exhaust end of the tube to clear spittle, dirt and moisture from the tube. If problems persist, you might have to remove the reed and clean it thoroughly.

When to Use Closed-Reed Calls

As mentioned, closed-reed calls are easy to operate and favored by hunters with less experience. Volume is regulated by how much air you blow through the call and how much you use your hands to baffle the end of the tube. But if you want to get a variety of sounds, you will have to carry more than one call. Large calls produce more volume and lower pitches, while smaller calls produce higher-pitched sounds and less volume.

If you'll be hunting big country or broken terrain, and will need a lot of volume to have any chance of a predator hearing you, then start with a closed-reed call to try to reach out to where the predators are hiding.

wood, plastic and metal. Each material affects the tonal quality of the call. Calls come in a variety of sizes and shapes that affect pitch and the amount of volume that can be generated. Generally speaking, smaller calls produce higher-pitched sounds and less volume, while larger calls generate more raspy lower tones and more volume.

Closed-reed calls are extremely durable and easy to use. They are favored by those new to the sport.

That is not to say that many seasoned predator hunters do not use these calls. Most veteran callers carry a supply of both open- and closed-reed calls and let the circumstances of the stand, weather, terrain and other factors dictate which tube they use.

There are a good number of closed-reed calls on the market including those offered by the Johnny Stewart Wildlife Call Company, Burnham Brothers, Primos, Thompson Calls and others.

*The metal reed of a closed-reed call is fully contained within a plastic, wooden or metal tube. To use a closed-reed call, follow these steps: **1)** Hold the call between your thumb and fingers. **2)** Place your lips over the end of the call, and **3)** cup one or both hands over the end of the call. Open and close your hands to vary the volume of the call. Use smaller closed-reed calls for high-pitched sounds and larger calls for lower sounds.*

ELECTRONIC CALLERS

Gerry Blair and I had been hunting the Arizona high-desert region near Wickenburg for the better part of three days, trying to obtain footage for a fox hunting video. And even though that part of the country is teeming with furred critters of every sort, we were batting a big fat zero.

We had called up a few nervous coyotes, a 5X5 desert mule deer and a troop of squawking crows. We had seen a bobcat in the pickup's headlights early one morning on the way to the stand and had even called a sounder of the desert "pigs" called javelinas shotgun close, but not one gray fox.

We had been giving it our best efforts, Gerry on his favored Thompson closed-reed and TallyHo open-reed calls, and me on a high-pitched Wiley cottontail tube. The gray foxes couldn't have cared less.

We had done death march after death march into the ragged country the little predators call home—the kind of terrain no self-respecting coyote would venture into. Stand after stand produced nothing. We had left the Johnny Stewart MS512 cassette caller in the truck; quite honestly, neither of us wanted to carry it.

Electronic callers add versatility to your calling repertoire, which often translates into hunting success.

Gerry and I agreed that it was time for a change. We drove to our next location, and after digging around in the back of the pickup for a few minutes, found the cassette player buried under who knows what-all. A quick check of the battery and we were off with regained optimism.

The next setup overlooked a brushy dry wash, and the sounds of a gray fox pup in a considerable amount of anguish replaced the plaintive rabbit cries that we had previously been using.

Not 10 minutes into the stand, a large male gray fox crested the hill on the opposite side of the wash and charged the call, tail held high, coming to within 10 steps of Gerry's bootstraps.

That calling episode punctuates the need to be versatile, especially when things are not going your way. For whatever reason, the foxes were not responding to food-source sounds on that hunt. Perhaps there was plenty of prey available and they weren't motivated to respond, or maybe the area had seen considerable calling pressure and the foxes were wary of the repetitive rabbit calls. I don't know.

But I do know that by remaining optimistic and digging deep into our bag of tricks, Gerry and I were able to turn that hunt around. By switching from food-source sounds to those that appealed to the fox's territorial instincts and curiosity, we salvaged a trip that was going from bad to worse.

Electronic callers are effective because they use

Gray foxes that won't come to food source sounds can sometimes be lured by the sound of gray fox pups in distress.

actual recorded animal sounds that predators are accustomed to hearing in the wild. This gives the caller authenticity, versatility and the confidence of knowing that the sounds he is using are genuine.

There are several types of electronic callers on the market utilizing different technologies. The Johnny Stewart Wildlife Call Company (now owned by Hunter's Specialties), Hunting Buddy and Lohman Game Calls all make cassette tape machines that are ruggedly built for field work.

Burnham Brothers Call Company markets a digital player that utilizes electronic chips programmed with four different sounds. These are actually simulations of real animal sounds and repeat every few seconds. And while they might sound repetitive to the hunter, the predators don't seem to mind.

More recently, some companies are using compact disc technology as a new format to record and play calling sounds.

There are a number of circumstances under which electronic callers give you an edge over mouth-blown calls. Electronic callers provide flexibility and adaptability to seasoned callers and instill confidence in those new to the game. Any serious predator hunter would be remiss not to have an electronic caller and a bunch of recorded sounds in his bag of tricks.

Versatility

Plain and simple, these calls and the melange of recorded animal sounds available make the electronic howler more versatile than the hunter who relies solely on conventional mouth-blown calls. The ability to use a wide variety of sounds—both food-related and territorial—means that you can cover a wider spectrum of behavioral traits associated

Where white-tailed deer are a favorite prey species for larger predators, a fawn-in-distress tape might bring them running.

with hunting predators. And an electronic caller will give you an edge in heavily called areas, where you might have to try two or three sounds before you find one that predators are attracted to or, at the least, less suspicious of.

Gerald Stewart says that electronic callers can also provide the flexibility needed to continually hunt predators where you have a restricted amount of land.

"When you have a limited area to hunt, you need to be able to go back to the same areas you've already hunted and remain productive," he says. "Electronics give you the option of mixing and matching sounds and keep you from educating predators. While mouth calls can be very effective under the right conditions, if you continue to use the same call stand after stand, your production will eventually diminish."

"It's like the old fisherman's tackle box," Gerald says. "He might have 25 different lures of various colors and styles. Sometimes, a topwater bait

Electronic callers (left) will give you an edge in heavily hunted areas, where you might have to try several different sounds (such as for a fawn, below) before you find a sound that works.

Armed with an electronic caller, a hunter can concentrate on getting a good shot at called animals rather than on trying to produce the "right" sounds.

centrate on handling called animals rather than on trying to produce the "right" sounds.

Taped animal sounds can also serve as a teaching aid. By listening to actual animal vocalizations and then replicating those sounds on various mouth calls, the beginner can use the tape machine as a tutorial for learning how to produce the proper sounds and cadence for calling predators.

Volume & Control

Electronic callers have the horsepower to deliver volume, and to control that volume efficiently. This can be beneficial under a number of conditions. One is wind. Nothing will knock the punch out of a mouth-blown call more quickly than wind. Machines are capable of producing enough volume to get your sound out there when the wind is whipping. Extra volume is also helpful when calling in heavy terrain, where the landscape and vegetation prevent sound from carrying very far.

Being able to control the output of volume makes you versatile in all kinds of calling conditions, in all types of terrain and for all sorts of animals.

Effective Sounds

Of course, electronic callers are only as good as the recorded sounds used with them. Fortunately, there is a wide selection available on cassette tapes and digital chips.

There are two different categories of sounds used to call predators: food-source and territorial sounds. A number of variables will often dictate which works best in a given situation.

Food-source sounds are generally the recordings of prey species in distress—those sounds you imitate with your favorite tube calls. However, recorded sounds can give you a much wider range of animals and the ability to mix and match sounds as you see fit. Some of the most popular food-source sounds include rabbits, birds, rodents and deer in distress.

Territorial sounds are often effective when predators are not responding to food-source sounds, or when you're calling in areas that have been heavily hunted. These sounds might include canine pups in distress, coyote vocalizations, and fighting sounds such as two gray foxes having at it. Territorial sounds

might be more appropriate and more effective than a spinner, or one color might outperform another. You have to remain flexible so you can change with the conditions. It's the same with predator calling. Electronic callers, with a variety of recorded animal sounds, give you that flexibility."

Confidence Builder

Using taped animal sounds boosts the confidence of novice callers, who might not be proficient with mouth calls. Recordings assure hunters that the sounds produced on tape or chip will call predators. Armed with an electronic caller, the hunter can con-

How to Use an Electronic Caller

Select your stand location, and position the speaker so that it will give off optimum coverage. If you suspect critters will approach from downwind, place the speaker upwind of where you will be sitting.

Select a tape, adjust the volume to a low setting and switch the machine on.

Let the tape run for a minute or more and then switch it off and wait for a couple of minutes. Some callers prefer to let the tape run throughout the stand.

Increase volume as the stand wears on, and if you get no response, you might want to switch from a food-source sound to a territorial sound before you call it quits.

It's as easy as one, two, three. **1)** *Find a good location, get settled in and set up your speaker.* **2)** *Select a tape, adjust the volume and …* **3)** *get ready for action.*

Hunting Equipment

are particularly effective during the mating season when canines and felines are staking out territories and diligently guarding their boundaries.

Electronic Caller Strategies

Electronic callers are simple to use. One of their best attributes is that you can position the speaker so that the sound draws the predator's attention away from you. You can accomplish this by stringing out a remote speaker 25 to 50 feet away from your setup. As an added touch, you might even want to use the speaker in conjunction with a decoy for added visual appeal.

Or, in the case of an electronic remote caller, you can position yourself a considerable distance downwind of the speaker. I have found this particularly effective with red foxes because of their inclination to circle the call.

The Bad with the Good

All news about electronic players isn't good, however, and I would be remiss not to mention their shortcomings.

Electronic callers and the tapes, chips and CDs they use can be costly, much more so than if you were to purchase several hand calls. And being machines,

they can fail at the most inopportune times. Batteries go dead, belts break, speakers blow, tapes break. Any one of these mishaps can put your player out of commission when you need it most. I never venture far from the truck without a backup mouth call in my pocket, and you shouldn't either.

Machines are somewhat heavy to lug around, and changing tapes or CDs in the middle of a stand can be noisy. Dirt, dust, moisture and subzero temperatures can all cause potential problems for the player.

Electronic callers might not be the right tool for all occasions, or even all hunters. But if you want to add versatility and adaptability to your best-laid plans, you should seriously consider purchasing an electronic player and a variety of good sounds.

Electronic callers can produce sounds that predators find irresistible, and might come running to.

HOWLERS

Leo Zentner, a rancher outside of Billings, Montana, had assured us that there were a bunch of coyotes hanging out in the hills not far from his outbuildings. He mentioned that he hears them howling and barking every night. So John Graham and I left the truck at first light and walked across a frozen pasture to our first setup of the morning.

We exchanged knowing looks as we crossed the pasture that was covered with canine tracks. Evidently, the coyotes were leaving the hills at night and coming down into the pasture to hunt for mice and rabbits, and then retreating into the breaks where they would hole up during the day. Hunkering low, we crested a rolling hill that overlooked a jagged creekbottom a quarter mile away, and settled in.

I began a series of rabbit calls and got an immediate response … two or three young coyotes barking excitedly. They were quickly cut short by the sharp warning barks of an adult male who seemed to be telling them to shut up and mind their manners. John told me later that he believed the dominant male was suspicious of the rabbit call and was warning the younger coyotes to sit tight.

John immediately got on the howler and received a couple of ill-tempered responses from the big dog. Then the motley crew went silent.

We were already about 20 minutes into the stand and I figured we were about to call it quits, that we had been had. John signaled that we were going to sit another 15 minutes or so. He was certain that the old male would eventually come down for a look. He was right; he usually is. Not five minutes later, the old dog zigzagged his way through the pasture, headed for our location.

I barked when the coyote was about 100 yards out and took the shot as he slowed to a stop. That bullet caught nothing but air,

By cupping your hands over an open-reed call, you can produce convincing coyote barks and howls.

Coyotes vigorously patrol the boundaries of their territories in search of intruders. Howling appeals to their territorial nature.

and some tricky off-hand shooting was required to topple the running dog. John and I shared in the fun.

John's knowledge of coyote behavior accounted for our success on that stand. He had seen this particular scenario before, and in a situation where most callers would have packed it in, we sat tight and played our final card, which happened to be an ace.

There are at least two good reasons—locating animals and then calling them in—why every serious predator hunter should own a howler. It is important to have at least a rudimentary understanding of how you can use coyote vocalizations to effectively locate and call coyotes.

Locating Calls

Since it is imperative that you call coyotes where there are coyotes, locating them is important. A howler or electronic siren can assure you that there are coyotes in the area and provide a starting point.

John says that this is particularly important in the West, where there are a lot of wide-open areas and most of it appears to be good coyote habitat.

"I'll travel a main county road or a ranch road early in the morning before daylight, blow the siren every two miles and note the location of different coyote pairs and families of coyotes," John says. "It's a very productive way of sizing up a place where you've never called before. Instead of spending a lot of time out hiking around looking for sign, you're actually getting a voice response. Sirens and howlers increase your odds for success."

Once you have located coyotes, you can devise an approach that will get you closer to their position. Once there, you can continue to attempt to call them in with a howler, a rabbit call or a combination of the two.

Young coyotes, because of their low social status, typically approach the call tentatively, on the lookout for any sign of danger.

A number of commercially crafted howlers on the market effectively mimic the coyote's vocabulary.

Howling Them In

John says that if he only had one call to use it would be a howler. He explained that by using coyote vocalizations, you're appealing not only to just a food response, but to the very social essence of the animal.

"I kill more coyotes each year with a howler than I do with the rabbit call," he says. "I really think it's an intrigue factor when they think there's another coyote in the area. There is a territorial response too."

Hunting Equipment

response for two reasons. One would be their tendency to defend their territory. On the other hand, they might just be intrigued that there is another coyote in the vicinity, especially if it's the time of year when they are looking for mates."

John says it's important that you attempt to interpret the meaning of the coyotes' vocalizations. "If you're hearing high-pitched howling and a lot of choppy barks, chances are they're not coming toward you. In that case, you can try to work in closer, howl again or use the rabbit call. You don't have to go in too close, just close enough for them to respond to the call. The important thing is, when they're howling, try to do the same type of howls back at them."

Howlers work well for calling dominant coyotes that vigilantly guard their territories.

Mature coyotes will seldom tolerate the presence of other adult coyotes within their domain.

"Say you're hunting an area that has a light population of coyotes, and their home ranges are large," he says. "They have very few other coyotes on the fringe of their territory, or it's the time of year when the young coyotes are beginning to disperse. In this situation, you can act as though you're an intruder infringing on their territory. This might get a

By sucking on the back of your hand, you can produce the soft squeaks made by rodents and grab the attention of any nearby predators.

CLOSE-UP CALLS

There is another category of calls used to coax uncooperative critters. These calls are helpful in situations when an animal responds to a call but, for whatever reason, hangs up just out of range or out of sight.

Close-up calls are designed to produce the soft rodent squeaks and squeals that predators find enticing. Small open-reed calls—such as the Johnny Stewart PC-3, which utilizes a metal reed tucked between two plastic channels that can be squeezed together to vary the pitch, or Ed Sceery's Rodent Coaxer, which is a small closed-reed call—are specifically fashioned for close encounters of the furred kind.

Some calls are fabricated from a rubber bulb that, when squeezed, forces air through a tiny reed. Hunters can hold them in one hand or attach them to the forend of their gun so calls can be operated in the ready position. Other calls utilize two flat strips of plastic with a rubber band positioned between them. This call is placed in the mouth and blown like a harmonica.

I often keep a single-reed diaphragm call—the type used to call turkeys—in my mouth while on a stand, knowing that if a customer hangs up I can

switch calls without causing much movement. Companies such as Quaker Boy Calls, Primos Calls and others, market diaphragm calls specifically designed for predator work.

With a little practice, these inexpensive calls can produce a wide variety of sounds that predators find appealing. I also favor them when hunting in extremely cold weather. I can keep them tucked in my warm mouth between calling sequences, and they continue to operate when other calls might be frozen tight.

Close-up "kissing" sounds can also be made using your mouth and lips. For close-up work, I emit high-pitch squeaks by forcing air between my pursed lips. Some hunters suck on the back of their hand to produce these sounds, or suck air through their lips as if they were calling their dog.

Electronic players are also capable of producing a variety of soft, tantalizing sounds. Burnham Brothers Compucaller, for example, has several sounds recorded on one digital chip, and switching from, say, a squirrel in distress to a lip squeak can be easily done with the flick of a switch. As for cassette players, there is a good selection of recorded rodent and bird sounds available. The only drawback is that you might have to switch sounds (i.e., change tapes) at an inopportune time.

I also use the lip squeak to alert a partner that I've spotted a critter and that he should get ready for action.

Bobcats often become mesmerized by the tantalizing sounds produced by close-up calls.

THE ART OF
COMPLETE CONCEALMENT

The use of camouflage and cover scents as hunting aids is, by no means, a new concept. Centuries ago, American Indians wore animal skins and other deceptive disguises to approach and kill wild game. They were also proficient at using decoys—often the skins of animals—to lure their quarry close.

To mask their human scent, they "bathed" in sweat lodges and rubbed their bodies with sage and other pungent herbs. Those early hunters recognized the need to fool all of the senses of those animals that they hunted for food and clothing.

Today's predator hunter has taken the art of concealment to an even higher level. Thanks to a technological boom in hunting equipment, hunters now have a wide selection of products available to deceive even the keenest of predators' sensory defenses. Camouflage clothing and equipment, cover and attractant scents, decoys, scent-elimination products: All help the modern predator hunter hide his lethal intentions.

A DETAIL GAME

Concealment, as it applies to hunting predators, entails much more than simply pulling on a set of camouflage clothing, dousing yourself with skunk musk and tromping off from stand to stand with a call in one hand and a rifle in the other. Those hunters who do not take extraordinary care to hide themselves from the probing eyes, noses and ears of the animals they hunt will most assuredly fail.

Wear camo from head to toe. Utilize cover scent and odor-elimination products. Keep your clothing free from foreign odors. Use the wind to your advantage. All this plays a significant role in deceiving the predator just long enough to turn the hunter into the hunted. But complete concealment for the purpose of luring predators shotgun-close entails much more—it requires that you attain complete stealth.

Predators are extremely sensitive to movement and sound. They make their living by detecting any extraneous sound or movement on the landscape and quickly assessing whether it translates to danger or their next meal. They rarely question their senses, and any inkling of threat sends a predator quickly on its way.

Slamming truck doors, talking, walking noisily and fidgeting on stand will render your concealment efforts useless. The best camo patterns available, the most pungent cover scents and the most appealing lures are no substitute for good hunting skills.

Always assume your next customer is waiting just out of sight. Sneak to and from each stand as quietly as possible and, once settled in, sit like a sniper throughout the complete sequence on the setup.

Finally, I feel compelled to mention attitude, for it is vital that you approach each and every stand with a genuine sense of optimism that comes with the confidence of knowing that the methods you are employing work. This, of course, is built on each success you experience while in the field. Never become discouraged, even when your best efforts fail to produce any positive results.

Only when you are armed with the assurance that the techniques and tactics you are employing are sound, the equipment that you have selected is exemplary and you are confident in your camouflage,

If your concealment is not complete, this is a view you might have to get used to.

will you have the fortitude to sit as still as a mountain throughout each setup. Only then will you reap the rewards of complete and unadulterated concealment.

COMPLETE CAMOUFLAGE

One of my favorite childhood games was hide-and-seek. Throughout the summer, I would rendezvous with the neighborhood gang outside my family's home at twilight. The object of the game was to hide from whoever was "it" and then sneak in to touch the sanctuary of the fieldstone chimney, which served as the "goal," without getting tagged.

The "keeper of the goal" had to locate one of the hiding kids and tag him or her while protecting the chimney from those "hiders" who were lurking nearby in the shadows.

Whoever was tagged before they reached the security of the chimney would, in turn, be "it" for the next round.

White camo patterns smattered with subtle grays, browns and blacks help break up the hunter's outline when calling in wintry conditions.

that goal. We hide in the bushes, predators seek us out and we complete the ambush.

Match the Cover

Years ago, there was little variety in the camo used to hunt predators—basically half-a-handful of army surplus patterns. Today, predator hunters have a vast selection of camo patterns and clothing styles to choose from. There are not only designs to blend with every conceivable terrain, but also materials that will keep you comfortable and quiet no matter what weather conditions you are hunting in.

Even though predators see the world in shades of blacks, grays and whites, use those earth tones—browns, greens and grays—that best match the country you are hunting. This will provide the identical shades of gray that predators are accustomed to seeing in their natural environment. In other words, you won't stand out as a foreign object as they scan the countryside for danger.

Those Northern hunters who must often hide in snow banks should, naturally, wear white clothing that matches that environment. However, those white camo patterns smattered with subtle grays, browns and blacks do a much better job of breaking up the outline. Even the most bleak wintry landscapes are rarely white on white.

To enhance the effectiveness of your camo, set up to utilize its full potential. That means backing up against vegetation and turf that best matches the patterns you are wearing, as well as selecting those areas nestled in the shade. And sit still! The best camo in the world will be rendered useless if you fidget.

Dress in Layers

If I anticipate a change in the weather, I wear two or three layers of camouflage clothing. Typically, temperatures change during the day and I want to be able to add or shed clothing while remaining totally camouflaged and comfortable.

And I also want to remain dry, which means the outer layer of clothing is usually waterproof or water-resistant to some degree. Even if it isn't raining, the ground and vegetation can be very moist early in the morning and your clothing should guard against the

I can still remember how my heart would race when I was being stalked by "it." I would remain as still as a rock and quiet as a mouse until the last moment, when I realized that I had been discovered. Then I would make a mad dash for the goal in hopes of getting there first.

I'm sure you can see the correlation I'm attempting to make here, given the fact that this chapter is about concealment and how it applies to predator hunting. We use stealth and ambush to fool the sensory defenses of the predators we stalk, and we rely heavily on a plethora of products to help us achieve dreaded soggy butt. I also carry a camouflaged seat cushion to keep me high and dry and to soften the hard ground.

Carry a couple different weights of camo gloves and face masks too, so that they can be changed as weather conditions and temperatures change.

Complete Coverage

Always go for complete coverage. In addition to full body camo including a long-sleeved shirt, pants, jacket and boots, wear a camo cap, face mask and gloves so that no skin is left exposed. Skin is highly reflective and any movement will be amplified if skin is left uncovered. It's also a good idea to have all of your peripherals camo'd, such as your firearms, shootings sticks, scopes, binoculars and so on.

The Night Shift

Camouflage clothing is not necessary when you are calling under the cover of darkness. However, it is important that you wear dark clothing. There is always some ambient light present at night—stars, moon, distant towns—and light-colored clothing will reflect those light sources. Conversely, wear white or light-colored clothing when hunting in snowy conditions during the night.

So when you play hide-and-seek with local predators, remember: If they are able to find any chink in your armor, any flaw in your concealment, you will be rendered to a terminal state of "it" and be left holding home base without any company.

PLAYING THE WIND

Concealing yourself from a predator's visual and auditory defenses often is not enough. Canines hunt with their noses, and are very adept at pinpointing the exact location of food or danger by analyzing the

Complete camouflage means leaving no reflective skin exposed. Be sure to wear a face mask and camo gloves for the best concealment.

tantalizing smells that travel the air currents.

Coyotes suspiciously approach a call, circling downwind as they near the source of the sound, especially if they suspect any danger. Red foxes generally travel downwind at a comfortable distance, making sure all is well before they commit to the call. Most gray foxes charge the call and circle only after they have arrived close to the source of the sound. All canines use the wind and their noses to determine if the approach is safe and to detect any inkling of danger.

Gerald Stewart and I discussed this characteristic on a predator hunt we shared in his home state of Texas. A pair of hard-charging gray foxes had shown up in the first minute of a stand and Gerald had toppled the female while her mate, who was cautiously

circling downwind, escaped in the heavy cover of some cedar bushes.

"A fatal characteristic of gray foxes is that most of the time they come in and use their eyes before they use their nose," Gerald explained. "For this reason, most hunters refer to them as either 'stupid' or 'aggressive.' But it's just the nature of the way they hunt."

"Coyotes, on the other hand, go downwind, utilizing thick brush like we have here," he said, pointing to the heavy cedar bushes that surrounded us, "and often smell what's happening before they see what's happening. If all is well, they approach the call from a downwind position."

Red foxes are masters at using the wind, a product of their paranoid disposition, and an indication of the low position they occupy on the food chain. I have hunted red foxes in North and South Dakota,

Montana, Minnesota, Indiana and Wisconsin, and I have noticed that they often circle several hundred yards downwind, using their nose, eyes and ears to detect any danger before committing to the call. Occupying a lower rung on the food chain requires that these small predators exercise extreme caution when approaching what might turn out to be a larger predator on a fresh kill.

The common thread here is that all these predators utilize the wind to some degree to analyze each situation they encounter. And it is this defense that you will have to break if you are going to be successful at calling them.

Setting Up for the Wind

Ideally, you would always set up with the wind in your face or drifting lazily from the right or left. This

Try to position yourself so that any approaching predator has to expose itself if going downwind. Always select locations where the terrain or vegetation funnels animals where you want them to go.

requires that you anticipate the direction from which predators will approach the call. To accomplish this, I try to position myself so that there is some sort of obstruction to my back to "force" them into the shooting lanes I have chosen. I try not to give predators the option of circling downwind. This could mean setting up with your back to a large body of water, an expansive field, a sharp cliff—anything that might funnel them so that the wind is in your favor.

If I'm hunting in hilly country, I often set up about two-thirds the way up a hill, where I have a good view of the downwind shooting lane. With an accurate rifle on a steady rest, I am able to get the drop on those animals circling to catch my scent.

Windy Conditions

Too much wind negatively impacts calling success. If the wind velocity is more than 15 mph or so, you might consider staying home and finding something more productive to do with your time.

There are three reasons why calling is difficult on windy days. First, sound does not carry as far and you will have a difficult time producing enough volume to be heard. Second, predators are less likely to respond to calls because wind reduces the effectiveness of their senses and they are reluctant to risk exposing themselves to danger. And finally, predators often hole up during windy conditions, opting to wait for better weather before resuming the hunt.

If you have no choice but to call on windy days, be mindful that animals generally head for heavy cover when winds are whipping. Select stands that overlook landscape features like creekbottoms, ravines and timber. And call loudly. With a little luck you might have a customer come out to take a look.

In hilly country, set up partway up a hill for better visibility downwind.

Hunting Equipment

COVER SCENT & SCENT ELIMINATION

If you were always set up to utilize the wind so that animals always approached from the upwind position, you would never need to worry about scent control. In fact, you should plan your stands so that you achieve that goal as often as possible. But, alas, there is never a guarantee that the predators you call will play by your rules. Rather, they will try to foil you at every turn.

Since most predators, especially canines, have a heightened sense of smell, it behooves the dedicated hunter to do his best to fool those sensitive noses whenever possible. There are a couple of ways that this can be accomplished: You can cover up the human odor that animals find so objectionable, or you can eliminate the problem.

Cover Scents

One of the most practical means of controlling your odor is to use a masking agent. The one most commonly employed by predator hunters is skunk musk, but some hunters also use red fox or raccoon urine, both of which have very pungent odors.

I generally carry several 35mm film canisters

Cotton balls soaked with skunk musk or fox urine effectively block human scent. Store them in 35mm film canisters during transport.

containing balls of cotton that I have soaked with skunk musk or red fox urine. While the plastic containers will not completely seal in the smell of the musk, they make it manageable as long as you are outdoors. I generally transport them in the back of the pickup when moving from stand to stand, and discard them at the end of the day.

At the stand, I simply remove the lids and place the containers 10 or 20 yards downwind of my position. When I'm ready to leave, I replace the lids on the containers and transport them to the next setup.

One of the handiest items I've come across is a product that utilizes a chemical reaction between two elements that produces a synthetic version of skunk musk—and a convincing one I might add. The chemicals are odorless until they are combined, so they can be transported or stored without the acrid odor of skunk following you around like a dark cloud.

Scent Control

If you really want to get extreme about controlling your human scent, there are products on the market to help you achieve that goal. Camouflage clothing (like that marketed by ScentLok, Whitewater Outdoors, Browning and others) utilizes activated charcoal to absorb human odor. Activated charcoal is the strongest, most effective absorbent material there is. It is commonly used in industrial applications and in household water filters. It is breathable, non–heat-retentive and allows moisture to pass through. Yet it filters out all organic compounds (scent molecules).

There are also odor-free sprays, shampoos and soaps, such as those made by the Wildlife Research

Center, that eliminate unwanted human odor by killing the bacteria that cause odor. Simply wash up with the soap and shampoo and then spray your outer clothing and you are in business.

Store your clean, scent-free hunting clothes in a clean container and only remove them just prior to the hunt. I use a garbage bag and spray my clothes with scent eliminator and then seal them up until I am ready to use them.

It's also important not to track unwanted odors to the stand with you. I've had coyotes turn nearly inside out when they hit the same trail that I walked on to get to the stand. Boots should, at the very least, be clean of foreign odors. If you want to take it a step further, spray the outside of your boots with a liquid odor eliminator and use scent-absorbing powder on the inside of your boots.

Some of these scent-control measures might seem extreme, and I'll be the first to admit that I don't always take such great precautions to cloak my presence when I'm hunting predators. I generally use cover scent at the stand and am always cognizant of wind direction. But if I'm hunting an area where I know the predators have been pressured, it's good to know that I can take the next step in scent control and use the mentioned products to render myself nearly undectable to those incredible noses.

Canines hunt with their noses. If you hope to fool a coyote, you must first fool its nose.

Hunting Equipment

HUNTING THE GRAVEYARD SHIFT

Many predators work the graveyard shift to avoid human encounters and hunt prey species that are abundant at night. This is especially true in the East, where human population densities are high and animals sneak out after humans' bedtime to forage for food. In many regions of the South, where temperatures can be blistering hot during the day, prowling in the relative coolness of night is more necessity than option.

Those animals that hunt at night are well adapted to do so. Not only do they rely on their acute olfactory and auditory senses, just as they do during the day, but they are equipped with eyes that are capable of turning the dim ambient light of night into lighter shades of grays. What might appear as pitch black to a human, more likely appears to be dim light to a nocturnal animal. The reason lies in the structure of the eye itself.

It's in the Eyes

Nocturnal animals' eyes are larger than ours. They also open more widely and are able to gather more available light. Further, many nocturnal eyes are designed to amplify the amount of light that reaches the retina. A feature called a tapetum reflects light that has already passed through the retina *back through* the retina, giving the light another chance to strike the light-sensitive rods, which detect motion and transmit basic visual information to the brain.

The tapetum is the reflection you see at night when you shine a light in an animal's eyes. Interestingly, not all animals reflect the same color of light. In fact, you can often identify what animals you are looking at by the color of the reflection.

Hunters who want to take advantage of heightened predator activity must also burn the midnight oil, or hunt those crepuscular hours just before sundown and after sunset. And while night hunting might only serve as an option in areas where predator populations are high and human occupancy low—where critters are amply called during the day—it might be your only recourse in areas where animals are completely nocturnal.

Night Life

Some timid predators become bold at night, gaining confidence under the cloak of darkness. Those that are reluctant to come to the call during the day exhibit a brave side of their nature during the night, often running up with unadulterated courage to investigate the source of the tantalizing screams that might mean a late supper.

To capitalize on the darker nature of predator hunting, those who venture afield after dark must leave the comfort of the recliner and scream like banshees when more sensible people are home, tucked away warm in bed. They must forgo social graces and become the recluse of the night. They must distance themselves from friends and family.

In states where it is legal, calling predators at night can be exciting and productive. And it can open up rich pockets of fur that are difficult to tap during the day. Very little extra gear is needed, except a good light for illuminating the predator's eyes. Skills you use to call daytime predators are just as effective at night. Fewer hunters venture out at night. In those areas where you might run into com-

The Nocturnal Eye

Predators that hunt the night shift have eyes that are adapted to amplify the amount of light that reaches the retina. A feature called a tapetum reflects light that has already passed through the retina back through it, giving the light another chance to strike the light-sensitive rods. The rods detect motion and transmit visual information to the brain.

Hunting Equipment

petition during the day, especially on public land, you will likely have the run of the property by night.

So why limit yourself to hunting during the day when you can pull a double shift and double your pleasure? Try working the graveyard shift and see if it doesn't add a dark side to your predator hunting adventures. Here's how.

LIGHTS & OTHER NIGHTTIME TOOLS

Equipment used to call predators at night is nearly identical to that used during the day, with the exception of lights. Calls, cover scent, guns and ammo are all standard provisions day or night.

Your choice of gear and how you use it will be affected by many of the same variables as during the day: the species of animals you are hunting, the type of terrain you will be hunting in, the length of the shot, the weather, and other factors.

Each calling situation might require a different approach in regard to equipment and techniques. For instance, if you are calling raccoons, bobcats or gray foxes in a brushy wash or riverbottom, you might be best served by a wide-angle spotlight and a shotgun. On the other hand, if you're hunting red foxes or coyotes in the wide-open prairies or the edges of expansive agricultural fields, you might opt for a spotlight with a more intense, focused beam and a flat-shooting rifle topped with a high-quality scope designed to gather light.

Always consider the type of hunting you will be doing and under what conditions, and then equip yourself accordingly.

Night Lights

Spot and shooting lights come in a variety of designs including heavy-duty flashlights, small 6-volt lights that are handheld or mounted to the top of a gun, and heavy-duty 12-volt spotlights capable of turning night into day.

The best lights generally provide 100,000 to 400,000 candlepower and come with variable-control rheostats and attachable red and amber lenses. Lights with variable controls allow you to use the least amount of light needed to illuminate the animals's eyes without alarming them. Some hunters use the coal miner–type lights that mount to a cap to keep their hands free.

Predators are far less sensitive to red and amber light than they are to bright white beams. Red and amber lights are less intense than white lights and are less likely to spook nervous animals. Foxes and coyotes seem to react differently to the spotlight. Foxes seem oblivious to red light while coyotes are more likely to hang up at a safe distance or look elsewhere for the evening's meal.

Spotting and shooting lights come in a variety of designs and models. The best generally provide 100,000 to 400,000 candlepower, come with variable-control rheostats, and offer attachable red and amber lenses.

Nighttime Optics

There are several options when considering what optics to use at night. Several manufacturers offer scopes with lighted reticles that make aligning the crosshairs on the predator's eyes a simple task. Other scopes utilize large objective lenses to gather sufficient ambient light to make shooting at night possible. If you want to go to the extreme, there are night-vision scopes available that use military-like technology. Small spotlights, with or without red filters, can be mounted on top of any scope to be used at the point of kill.

High-power scopes with large objective lenses draw the needed ambient light to make low-light shooting possible.

For shotguns, there are lighted beads that attach to the raised rib of the barrel, and electronic-dot scopes that feature a dim red light centered in a 1-inch tube. Some of these have low-power magnification. You'll want to adjust these red-dot scopes to their lower settings. If the red dot is too intense, it is difficult to pick up the animal's silhouette in the dark tube. Laser sights are also an option where they're legal.

Other Considerations

Your choice of firearm should not only reflect the type of animals you are hunting, but it should also be safe to discharge at night when you cannot see far beyond the beam of your artificial light. If I'm hunting in fox country and am not likely to encounter coyotes, I generally carry a .22 Win. Mag. for shots out to 75 yards or so. More often, though, I attempt to draw foxes within 40 yards and rely on a tightly choked 12 gauge loaded with No. 6s or No. 4s.

In coyote country, the .17 Rem., .222 Rem., .223 Rem., or similar calibers are generally good choices. They are not as loud as some of the larger calibers and the lighter bullets don't carry quite as far.

Predators will circle downwind at night just as they do during the day, so use cover scent to mask your odor and set up with the wind in your favor.

Working the graveyard shift can add excitement and variety to the predator-hunting game. Those who get a charge out of hiding in the bushes imitating a predator's supper will get an extra kick out of catching them on their way to the refrigerator for a midnight snack.

TECHNIQUES FOR NIGHT HUNTING

In regard to technique, there is little difference between calling during the day or night. Stand selection, calling sequence, scent control and all the other elements that make daytime hunting productive must also be implemented when night calling.

The Basic Night Plan

Drive to your location and quietly get out of the truck, being careful not to slam doors or make any unnecessary noises. Walk quietly—no talking—to your setup, using as little light as possible. Just as you would during the day, use available cover to conceal your movements.

Once you are on stand, settle in and use the same calling techniques and sequences that you would use during daytime, whether you're using mouth calls or an electronic caller. If you're hunting with a buddy, one of you can operate the light and do the calling while the other stays at-the-ready with the gun. Trade places at every other stand so that you both get a chance at shooting.

If you're hunting alone, it gets a little trickier. You'll have to operate the light, call and shoot. You can accomplish this by using an electronic caller, which you can leave running, and by mounting a light to the top of your gun. Sometimes I use a diaphragm call at night, which allows me the use of both hands to operate the light and keep the gun at the ready.

The red beam of the spotlight does not seem to bother most predators, and you can leave it on for the duration of the stand. Sweep the beam from side to side in slow arcs, keeping it constantly moving.

You do not want the direct beam of the light to frighten the animal, so keep the outer edge of the light's halo just touching the ground.

If you pick up eyes in the outer beam, keep them illuminated as the animal approaches the call. Once you feel that the critter is in close enough for the shot, direct the main intensity of the beam on the animal. This should signal your partner that it's time to take the shot.

Begin each calling sequence with the light at a low setting and increase the intensity of the beam throughout the stand if nothing shows up.

Hunting from the Truck

Predators seem to be less fearful of vehicles at night. In fact, where it is legal, many callers hunt from the truck bed or special platforms built on top of their trucks. This type of hunting is especially popular in Texas, where I've shared several predator hunts with Gerald Stewart.

Gerald does a considerable amount of night call-

Gray foxes, which are typically bold during the day, are even more fearless at night under the cloak of darkness.

ing and says it can be very productive and extremely exciting. His Suburban is specially rigged for night calling, with a large platform and swivel chairs on top.

"It's a common way to hunt predators in states where it's allowed," Gerald told me. "Some states allow it from vehicles and some states don't. Gray foxes in particular seem to get even more aggressive under the cover of darkness. We've actually had them run right under the truck and expected to have them come out with grease all over their backs," he laughed.

Gerald says it's important, even when using a red lens, to leave the hot bright spot up off the ground and use the outer halo of the light to pick up their eyes until they're in shooting range. He also says that sometimes you will have to use the white light and a scoped rifle for coyotes because they can be reluctant to come in.

"Generally speaking, gray foxes come closer and coyotes stay farther out," Gerald says. "Chances are you'll need to illuminate coyotes more for a scoped shot."

Light of the Moon

The best nights to call using artificial lights are those that are calm and dark—a new to half moon or, preferably, before or after the moon has set.

If I'm hunting under the light of the moon, without a spotlight, I prefer to do so under a half moon, which provides plenty of light for shotgun work. Predators seem hesitant to expose themselves if the moon is too bright, so they hug the cover as they circle the sound.

Hunting at night has its inherent dangers. Always positively identify your target before shooting, and

Predators seem to be less fearful of vehicles at night (top). In fact, where it is legal, many callers hunt from the truck bed or special platforms built on top of their trucks. In states where it's legal, hunters go to great pains to customize their trucks for predator hunting (bottom).

know what lies beyond it. Occasionally, deer and domestic livestock will approach the call out of curiosity. If you are not sure of your target, never take the shot. It's always better to be safe than sorry.

Hunting Equipment

DECOYS FOR PREDATOR HUNTING

*H*unters of every sort have long used confidence decoys to lure waterfowl, turkeys, pronghorns, deer and a host of other animals into effective sure-kill range. These visual aids, used in tandem with various calls and lures, provide the means to effectively fool even the most wary animals. Not only do decoys appeal to territorial and breeding instincts, they play on the inherently gregarious nature of most animals.

But while decoys are commonly used to hunt prey species, many hunters don't realize that they can also be equally effective for grabbing and holding the attention of predators.

Decoys might not be practical, or even effective in every situation, but there are times when their use will give the hunter a needed edge. My friend Mark Miller and I were hunting coyotes in southern Indiana a few years back, trying our best to obtain footage of an Eastern kill for an instructional predator-hunting video.

Coyote sign was abundant on the property we had secured, but we were having a difficult time drawing the paranoid predators out of the heavy cover where they spent the majority of their time. I suspect many of them were responding to the call, but circling downwind out of sight, where they picked up our scent.

One particular setup had us returning time and again because of the amount of sign in the immediate area. It was evident that coyotes were mousing in a nearby grown-over clear-cut, bordered on all sides by heavy timber. Our only option for setting it up was to position ourselves downwind on a dim two-track road that bordered the west side of the clear-cut. We hoped to call a coyote out onto the road and then hold it there long enough for a shot.

A quick trip to the store provided the small stuffed animal that would serve as a decoy. We sneaked into the setup about an hour before sunset, prime time for coyotes on the early prowl. I placed "Wolfy" in the middle of the road where he was highly visible, and Mark and I settled in for the ambush.

Mark cranked up the electronic player and the plaintive cries of a gray fox pup in distress filled the air. About 20 minutes into the stand, a young coyote stepped up onto the road and looked toward the call. The furry makeshift decoy immediately grabbed his attention, freezing him like a well-trained pointing dog. Mark made the 200-yard shot and Wolfy received credits in the video. Had we not used a decoy on this setup, it is likely that the coyote would not have paused long enough on the road for the shot.

APPEALING TO THE EYES

As the sport of predator hunting evolved, the hunter's bag of tricks grew larger. In the early days, the 1950s and '60s, the average hunter appealed mainly to the predators' sense of hearing, using various hand and electronic calls to lure them close. Then in the 1970s and early '80s, people began discovering the advantages of using scent attractors and cover scent to account for predators' keen sense of smell. And then in the late 1980s and '90s, there was considerable growth and development in the use of decoys to appeal to a third major sense, predators' incredible eyesight.

Gerald Stewart is an advocate of using decoys when situations warrant, and says that they can be effective on all predator species. "Today, most wildlife callers try to appeal to animals' sense of hearing, smell and sight to lure or decoy them in closer," he says. "It seems more often you need to engage all three senses as they become more educated to commonly applied techniques, especially in areas that are heavily hunted. A decoy adds one more element of realism to the scenario you're attempting to create. It puts the animal more at ease and gives you those few extra seconds to get your gun around."

DECOY STRATEGIES

Decoys can be as simple as a feather that you twirl around in your fingers, to something as elaborate as a stuffed coyote or rabbit. Technology has even given us battery-operated decoys, like Rigor Rabbit from Feather Flex, which can be set to wiggle at appropriate intervals. If you choose to go a simpler route, you can hang either a tanned pelt over a bush or tie a feather on a string to attract the animal's attention, or use an inexpensive stuffed toy as Mark and I did.

Gerald says that feathers work particularly well on cats. "They say that curiosity killed the cat, and it couldn't be truer in the case of a feather hanging from a bush," he comments.

There are a wide variety of ways to set up when using decoys, Gerald says. You can use them to attract attention away from you, like by setting them

Elaborate decoys, like this white-tailed fawn, can draw the predator's attention away from the hunter to help provide close action.

out near the speaker of an electronic caller or off to the side to divert attention away from a calling hunter. Gerald often uses them to draw attention directly to the caller while a second hunter waits off to the side to ambush incoming animals.

"I actually set one of my favorite stuffed rabbits between my feet so I can move it if I see an animal approaching and I think it needs a visual stimulant," Gerald reveals. "And I have literally had coyotes come within four or five feet while I'm wiggling a feather between my fingers. This works particularly well in tighter cover when hunting with shotguns."

Veteran caller Gerry Blair also recognizes the value of using decoys under some circumstances and has gone as far as creating full-mount jackrabbits and coyotes for his calling purposes. Gerry explains that decoys work well because when a predator gets close to the source of the sound, it expects to see something. When it doesn't, it may become suspicious and leave in a hurry. Using a decoy makes the setup more realistic and often causes the predator to stick around those precious few seconds needed for the shot.

For optimum success, savvy predator hunters use all the tools at their disposal. While decoys might not work in all situations, they certainly have a viable place in your bag of tricks.

Hunting Equipment

Chapter Four

SURE-FIRE TACTICS FOR HUNTING PREDATORS

*I*t is said that experience is the best teacher, and it is this premise that cuts to the very essence of predator hunting. Each trip afield, each outing shared with a hunting buddy, each lesson learned ... all help the hunter better understand the many nuances that make calling predators exciting and enjoyable. Anyone who says that he has seen it all or done it all has more to learn than he can possibly imagine.

Like most hardened predator hunters, I have learned from the best: Wily Coyote, Bashful Bob and Fanciful Fox have all taught me the humility that goes along with the chase. They have provided the many failures that accompanied the successes. They have, all too often, left me sitting and scratching my head.

Remember, you are only visiting their reality. For them, the hunt is the very fabric of their existence. You are hunting on their turf, under their rules, in their backyard.

The following excerpts are accounts of some of my most memorable and educational times afield in the pursuit of predators. Of course, for every successful hunt that made the pages of this book there were many fruitless trips to be sure—too many to mention. But it's the relative frequencies of those successes and failures that build predator hunting character. Only when you can muster a positive attitude during times when success is evasive will you truly appreciate the times when success is finally at hand.

As I look back on all those times in the field and the memories my predator hunting mentors have provided, I better understand what continues to drive me to search for that elusive flash of fur.

HUNTING BUDDIES

Predator hunting gets in the blood. It replaces fighter T-cells, breaking down the immune system. In later stages, it weakens the mind and monopolizes rational thought. That's why, I suppose, some call it a disease.

Passion for hiding in the undergrowth, imitating a fox's or coyote's supper, grows with every trip afield—or whenever hunting compadres gather at local sporting goods stores or coffee shops to swap their adventure tales.

It's only reasonable, then, that most predator hunters have a favorite hunting buddy—one with whom they can share the details of each hunt, a kindred soul with shared realities. I'm lucky. I have several.

A COYOTE EAST OF THE RIVER

It has been my good fortune to hunt with Gerry Blair, Gerald Stewart, Larry O. Gates, Scott Huber, Doug Huston, John Graham, Mark Miller and too many more to mention here.

But when Mark Miller and I donned our favorite camo late one October and drove in silence to our predawn destination, we were on a purposeful mission that had little to do with our friendship or our passion for hunting coyotes. We were on a mission of ill intent.

This was strike three. The final countdown. The fat lady was on the final stanza and already thinking about the half-eaten donut waiting for her in the dressing room.

There was more at stake than simply building a few more memories. We had made an investment of time and money. Even our reputations were on the line.

Inclement weather, poor timing and bad luck had cooperated to make the field production of a predator-hunting video that we were working on a test of wills. It was a project 18 months in the making.

We had footage of several Western coyote kills in the vault, but the Eastern dogs were giving us fits. We felt that the video would lack legitimacy if we could not provide footage of a kill or two east of the big river.

Most callers have a favorite hunting buddy or two with whom to share the thrills and excitement of the hunt ... moments like this.

We were in prime coyote country, but capturing a kill on tape is rarely an easy undertaking, especially in the East where coyotes are generally nocturnal. So many things needed to go right. And Murphy's Law had been working overtime.

The $2,000 coyote (the time and travel I figure we had invested in it) broke cover in earnest. It wanted the rabbit badly and was willing to risk all for it.

Mark sat to my right at the ready, his .17 Rem. balanced on a Harris bipod. He readied himself further as the canine closed ground, braking to a loping bounce as it circled Rigor Rabbit, our decoy. My heart pounded as I watched the drama unfold through the lens of the video camera. Mark panned frantically to his left as the coyote made the pass. I did my best to mirror that movement.

That's when things went terribly wrong. Mark's bipod legs got hung up in the tall grass that broke his outline, and his first shot caught nothing but air. I watched in disbelief as the coyote ignored the loud report of the rifle and continued its run-by.

I barked. The coyote slowed and looked in my direction!

I barked again. The coyote pulled to a halt and stood stiff, hackles raised!

This was Mark's chance to redeem himself—our chance to accomplish what we had failed to do on previous trips to Indiana.

His second shot was true. The coyote spun around and departed at a dead run (literally). Mark finished the job with a well-placed bullet that hit the dog between the shoulders.

With the coyote down, we collectively sighed. I joined Mark for the retrieve and to shoot the footage that would occupy portions of the final video.

83   *Sure-Fire Tactics for Hunting Predators*

Two hunters means two sets of eyes, two guns and shared predator hunting knowledge and experience. This usually adds up to more efficiency in the field.

THE TWO-HUNTER ADVANTAGE

Like all good hunting buddies, Mark and I will forever cherish the precious moments of that stand. We will relive them over and over and, no doubt, embellish the details of the hard charge and near miss with each retelling.

For me, the best part of tandem hunting is enjoying the fellowship of another hunter; to share in the excitement and thrill of the hunt and to continually ask the rhetorical question: Did you see that? But there are, perhaps, more logistical reasons why a good hunt can be made better with a buddy along.

Two hunters means two sets of eyes, two guns and shared predator hunting knowledge and experience that add up to better stand selections and cooperative scheming. It means you have a doubly good chance of putting the hammer down on a hard-charging double if the opportunity presents itself ... or maybe even scoring the coveted hat trick.

Gerry Blair and I were on the tail end of a three-day high-desert hunt in Arizona—on the way back to the airport in Phoenix, actually. Gerry pulled the pickup to the side of the dusty road and turned in his seat. "Wanna try one more?" he smiled. I gazed out the window at an expan-

sive valley, scattered with mesquite, palo verdes and all sorts of other pokey plant life, that seemed to stretch to the western horizon. "Sure," I answered. We grabbed our stuff and made a short hike to a high vantage point and set up to do business.

To make a long story short, I called up a trio of eager coyotes that broke cover in earnest at 30 yards only 10 minutes into the stand ... single file ... hell-bent for rabbit.

Gerry rugged out the first two with his formidable 10 gauge and I caught the third with the .243 Win. as the coyote made a mad dash out the back door for home and Mother. Three coyotes called, three dead. A feat neither of us would have likely managed alone.

There are a good number of reasons to hunt buddy-style that have less to do with fellowship than efficiency. Here are a few examples.

Downwind Dilemma

Most predators have a tendency to circle downwind if they sense danger or are suspicious for any reason. I find this is particularly true of the inherently timid red fox. Many times, this translates into missed opportunities for the solo hunter.

The remedy, as you might have guessed, is teamwork. By positioning a second rifleman 50 to 100 yards downwind of the caller, you can successfully intercept those foxes or coyotes that use the wind to circle the source of the sound. I will mention here that it is a good idea to have a predetermined signal

The author, right, and Gerry Blair team up for a hat trick on a single stand.

Always watch the back door while hunting cats, because you never know who'll be watching you.

should a customer arrive. I usually purse my lips and emit a soft squeak to alert my partner. If I can't find a buddy to tag along, I often use an electronic caller (mine has a remote control) and position myself downwind of the sound source. Once I'm settled in, I simply turn on the machine and get ready for action.

Double Trouble

Another advantage of having two hunters on the stand is the added firepower. This is especially handy if more than one fox or coyote shows up at the stand. Oftentimes, when a group of coyotes responds to the call, they do so with the confidence that comes with numbers. This can make for fast and furious action, especially if the cover is tight.

Have an understanding that whoever is positioned on the right will shoot those predators to the right and vice versa. In broken terrain, one hunter should carry a

With the coyote's attention focused on the caller, the gunner is in prime position for the shot.

rifle to the stand should a stubborn customer hang up at a distance. The other can tote a shotgun loaded for bear for those up-front and in-your-face chargers. By optimizing your firepower on the stand, you have a much better chance of putting those hard-charging doubles, and even triples, in the fur shed.

Backdoor Bobcats

It is extremely important to watch the back door, especially when hunting cats. Oftentimes, predators will sneak to the sound of the call and turn up unexpectedly from any direction. Sometimes when I hunt with Gerry Blair, we position ourselves on the opposite sides of a hill, out of sight of each other. That way we can watch for circling animals, as well as have more shooting lanes covered.

While predator hunting might not be a spectator sport, adding a good buddy to the mix can add enjoyment and efficiency to the hunt. The next time you take to the field to chase predators, bring a friend along and double your fun.

CROSS-COUNTRY CRITTERS

*D*oug Huston turned in his saddle and smiled as a pair of song dogs exchanged pleasantries a half mile away. "They're ours," his grin widened. We had been zigzagging the broken terrain of the South Dakota Badlands on horseback for the better part of the day, but had not yet hung one "prairie wolf" from the saddle horn. We had seen about a dozen or so coyotes, but these January veterans were not easily fooled. Still, we had one last chance. The sun was sliding over the horizon as we nudged our horses and quietly shaved off the distance to the howling dogs.

"They're deep in that ravine," Doug leaned over and whispered as we climbed down from our mounts. We ground-hobbled the horses so they could munch the prairie flora in our absence and, hunkering over, we made our way to the edge of the draw. A small band of mulies crossed below us, spooked slightly by our approach. Quietly, we melted into the prairie landscape.

Doug crafted the long howl of a lonely coyote, hoping to get a friendly response. No dice. Terrified rabbit was next. The sound echoed in the broken contours of the landscape. The deer that had been hanging to our left scattered as the form of a lone canine disturbed the skyline, beelining toward us and the tantalizing screams. The dog appeared fixed on a rabbit dinner, but stalled 200 yards out to survey the situation. "Take him," Doug whispered.

I waited, sure the coyote would continue up the draw, offering a better shot in the waning light. My mistake. A slight breeze caressed the back of my neck and I knew that I had blown what might have been our only chance to dodge the skunk. The wind

Hunting the "outback" can put you in Wily's backyard, far away from roads and any hunting pressure.

had switched direction, blowing our scent straight down the draw. Our customer circled to the right and disappeared.

Doug got back on the TallyHo caller, but the coyote wasn't buying it. Just as we were about to call it quits, a second coyote appeared, working toward us in much the same manner as the first. This time when it stopped about 160 yards out to test the wind, I squeezed the trigger, sending 70 grains of death coyote-bound. My shot was echoed by a loud report to my left. I looked over at Doug who was smiling ear to ear. "Just making sure," he laughed.

We walked over to collect our prize and discovered the she-dog had received a double dose of lead poisoning. Although she was more dead than need be, we were relieved that the day had ended on a successful note. The full moon was just breaking the eastern horizon as we walked back to the horses. It was time to call it a day. We lumbered back to the trailer and loaded our gear. Tired, we headed for home.

TRAVEL ROUTES & FOOD SOURCES

Wandering into the "outback"—putting on miles across the countryside—can put the persistent predator hunter in Wily's backyard, where the crafty

canine might let down his guard just a bit. If you're not afraid to wear down the soles of your favorite hunting boots a little, stepping off the beaten path might provide the kind of action you're looking for. Predators, and the critters they hunt, acclimate to

Horses are not just for big game anymore, and they add much-needed mobility in the great expanses of the West.

Sure-Fire Tactics for Hunting Predators

When hunting cross-country, work into the wind, and stop to call every quarter mile or so.

human activity by avoidance. They become extremely nocturnal or seek remote locations where human encounters are minimal.

Having said that, I will add that predators are opportunistic feeders, and farms and ranches offer a substantial food source that cannot be overlooked. Where large tracts of land are prevalent, predators often hole up in secluded areas during the day, then wander out to forage for food under the cover of darkness. Daylight hunting near ranches or farms usually turns up lots of sign but little fur.

Mark Kayser, Mike Moody and I experienced such a situation during a coyote hunt in South Dakota a few years back.

From my vantage point overlooking the Bad River, I could see a good portion of the ribbon of ice that wound its way through the pasture directly below me, cutting into the distant hills. The coyotes were working the deep washes just out of sight, and I could only hope that the inquiring howls and barks I had sent would spark their curiosity and bring them in my direction.

An old male, hoarse with age, barked out a gravelly

warning, clearly infuriated by the presence of a strange voice within his domain. "Keep your distance, or else," he seemed to shout.

I answered with a tentative bark, then sat silent. After waiting 15 minutes, I glanced over at Mike, who was dug in about 30 yards away. A shrug of his shoulders signaled what I already knew—the stand was over. Apparently, the band of marauders had retreated to the hills where they would spend the remainder of the day. The old dog had decided not to press the issue. His territory, for now, was defended.

Silently, we walked back to the truck where we rendezvoused with Mark, who had been watching the other side of the ravine. He had seen a pair of coyotes making their way from the ranch back into the hills, but nothing within calling distance.

"We should have worked in behind them, farther back," Mark mumbled to the prairie wind as we climbed into the Suburban and fired up the heater. Warming my numb hands on the defroster, I listened to Mark second-guess our strategy.

"They hang around down here by the cattle at night and head up into the hills before first light.

We're going to have to get farther back to get a crack at 'em."

And that's just what we did. The next morning we hiked back into the rolling hills a few miles from the ranch. We called and killed two coyotes as they meandered to their daytime hangout. I found it interesting that these dogs, which were paranoid to the Nth degree when near the ranch, displayed a nonchalant attitude when back in the folds of their lair. Getting back into the hills not only put us on coyotes, it put us on receptive coyotes.

No matter what predator you are pursuing, hunt near food sources and determine predator travel routes to and from those sources. That way, you might be able to intercept them while they meander back to their daytime haunts. Early-morning glassing can help you determine what predators are doing and when. You might be surprised by how pre-

Pay attention to the location of predator food sources, like small rodents.

dictable they are, often taking the identical routes day in and day out at the same time each morning.

Winter food sources might be anything from rodents to winter-killed cattle to manure (yuck). Like any other animal, predators are creatures of habit, when undisturbed. If a food source remains constant and if they do not feel threatened, they will come back until it is depleted.

PLANNING YOUR ROUTE

One year, while hunting the Missouri Breaks in southeastern South Dakota, I embarked on a cross-country trek that put me deep in coyote country. Mike Moody followed me to where I parked my truck on a bluff overlooking the Old Missouri. He then drove me a half-dozen miles downstream, where he dropped me off about three hours before

Tailor your hunts to intercept predators traveling to and from food sources.

If you're hunting with a partner, you can leave one vehicle at one end of a large ranch or tract of public land, drive the second vehicle around to the opposite side, and hike-and-hunt your way back to the first vehicle.

It is also advisable to carry a small lunch and a container of water. Take your time and stop for a break now and again as needed.

USING MAPS

No matter where you go, there you are. And maps are invaluable tools for helping to decipher exactly where you are in relation to where you were and where you want to go. If you plan to take an overland trek for predators, maps can make the endeavor more productive and enjoyable.

A map might be something as simple as a rancher's scratched-into-the-ground layout of the major boundaries of his property, or as complex as a topographical plat showing every blemish on the landscape. Any map is invaluable for getting to know a piece of land. With map and compass, you can easily navigate unfamiliar territory and analyze which regions are most likely to hide the predators you hope to encounter.

sunset. Navigating the unfamiliar terrain was a breeze. All I had to do was keep the big river to my right as I zigzagged back to the truck.

That hike put me in country that had seldom, if ever, seen another predator hunter. Sure, the coyotes that hang out back there are persecuted when they venture onto nearby ranches, but when tucked into the folds of the breaks, they feel relatively at ease.

If you're hunting buddy-style, you can leave one vehicle at one end of a large ranch or tract of public land, drive the second vehicle around to the opposite side, then hunt your way back to the first vehicle. Work into the wind, stopping every quarter mile to call. If you will cover several miles, carry skinning equipment to rough-skin your critters and a backpack to carry out your fur.

A rough job is all that is required. I carry a sharp knife, a piece of rope for hanging the animal, latex gloves and a few small garbage bags. Strip the hide from the carcass, throw it in a garbage bag and into your backpack. Then get back to hunting. The fleshing and stretching can be done when you get home, or you can throw your skins in the freezer and finish them up at your convenience.

Maps and topos help you get acquainted with a piece of real estate before you even step foot on it.

Forest Service Maps

Maps are available, from public and private sources, that will help you get to know a piece of real estate before you hunt it. Free regional Forest Service maps are available from the Public Affairs Office of each region in the United States. You'll also find the U.S. Forest Service and its regional offices nationwide on the World Wide Web at www.fs.fed.us.

Region 1: Northern U.S. (Montana, northern Idaho, North Dakota, northwestern South Dakota)
200 E. Broadway St., Box 7669
Missoula, MT 59807
(406) 329-3089

Region 2: Rocky Mountain (Colorado, Kansas, South Dakota, eastern Wyoming)
11177 W. 8th Ave., Box 25127
Lakewood, CO 80255
(303) 275-5350

Region 3: Southwest (Arizona, New Mexico)
517 Gold Ave. S.W.
Albuquerque, NM 87102
(505) 842-3076

Region 4: Intermountain (Nevada, Utah, southern Idaho, western Wyoming)
324 25th St.
Ogden, UT 84401
(801) 625-5262

Region 5: Pacific Southwest (California)
630 Sansome St.
San Francisco, CA 94111
(415) 705-2874

Region 6: Pacific Northwest (Oregon, Washington)
333 S.W. First St.
Portland, OR 97204
(503) 326-2971

Region 8: Southern U.S. (Alabama, Arkansas, Florida, Georgia, Kentucky, Louisiana, Mississippi, North Carolina, Oklahoma, South Carolina, Tennessee, Texas, Virginia)
1720 Peachtree Road N.W.
Atlanta, GA 30367
(404) 347-2384

Region 9: Eastern U.S. (Illinois, Indiana, Iowa, Maine, Maryland, Massachusetts, Michigan, Minnesota, Missouri, New Hampshire, New Jersey, New York, Ohio, Pennsylvania, Rhode Island, Vermont, West Virginia, Wisconsin)
310 W. Wisconsin Ave. - Room 500
Milwaukee, WI 53203
(414) 297-3600

Region 10: Alaska
709 W. 9th St., Box 21628
Juneau, AK 99802
(610) 975-4111

Other Map Sources

The U.S. Outdoor Atlas & Recreation Guide
Houghton Mifflin Co.
215 Park Ave. S.
New York, NY 10003

Atlas & Gazetteer
DeLorme Mapping Co.
Box 298
Yarmouth, ME 04096
(800) 452-5931
www.delorme.com/atlases/atlasgaz.htm

BLM Surface Management Maps

The absolute best maps for locating public land and determining access to it are Bureau of Land Management (BLM) 1:100,000 scale topographic maps, also known as Surface Management Maps.

Most BLM land is west of the Missouri River, but the maps are available for all states. The BLM controls millions of acres of public land—much of it great for predator hunting—in the West.

These maps are detailed right down to specific, clear color keys that show land ownership not only of BLM land but also national forests, state forests and other public ground. You can locate a specific area to hunt predators on a map like this, make a plan for getting away from roads and two-tracks (unless new ones were forged since creation of the map) and get an excellent idea of the lay of the land and topographical features such as foothills, mountains, canyons, coulees, hillsides, flats, streams and springs. At the 1:100,000 scale, 1 inch on the map equals about 1.58 miles on the ground. These maps cost about $5 each.

Call the appropriate BLM office (see below for phone numbers and available URLs) for help in obtaining these maps. You'll start by ordering an index that will help you determine which maps to purchase. In some cases, if you know the county and/or hunting units you're interested in, the BLM personnel might be able to help you figure out which specific maps to get. You can also check out the BLM's Web site at www.blm.gov for more information and links to regional Web sites.

Before you head out to the field, you might want to check with local land management agencies to make sure there haven't been recent land sales and exchanges resulting in changed ownership status of lands. Most of these sales are taking place to "block up" larger tracts of public lands for the public to use, and you'll want to find out where these new and larger tracts are.

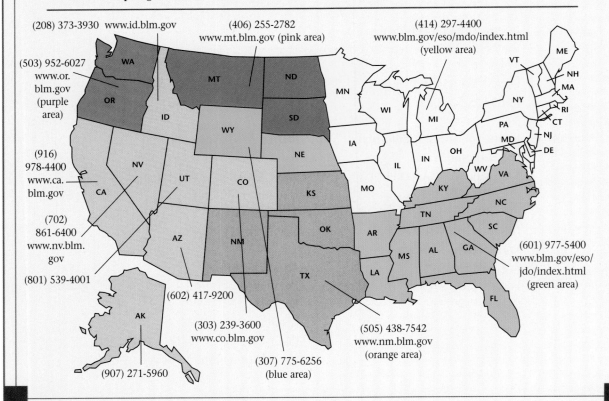

If you're into high-tech hunting, you can take outback hunting to a new level. With the advent of the handheld Global Positioning Systems (GPS) unit, navigating and plotting unfamiliar territory has never been easier.

GPS is a space-based triangulation system that uses satellites and computers to measure positions anywhere on Earth. By punching in a "waypoint" it is easy to navigate from one location to the next while recording specific landmarks and destinations.

A variety of GPS receivers are on the market, starting at less than $200. For the typical outdoorsman, a good GPS receiver should have the capability to track eight satellites and receive the GPS satellite signals through forest canopy and breaks in the terrain.

When turkey hunting in the Black Hills, I used a handheld GPS unit as a means of always knowing where my truck was. I would simply punch in my location each time I left the truck, and then use the GPS unit to navigate to and from that location.

You have to hunt predators where they are. And if that means hiking back into regions that are not easily accessible, so be it. The rewards will most often justify the added effort. Be sure to have map and compass as backups, should your modern technology go on the blink.

Handheld GPS units help you navigate your way back to the truck in unfamiliar territory.

Global Positioning System (GPS) Sources

T he availability of handheld Global Positioning System units has revolutionized the way many outdoorsmen navigate while afield. There are numerous models to choose from, ranging in price and capabilities. The following are some of the companies that offer handheld GPS units suitable for field use.

Garmin International
1200 E. 151st St.
Olathe, KS 66062
(913) 397-8200
www.garmin.com

Lowrance Electronics
12000 E. Skelly Dr.
Tulsa, OK 74128-2486
(800) 324-1356
www.lowrance.com

Magellan Systems Corp.
960 Overland Ct.
San Dimas, CA 91773
(909) 394-5000
www.magellangps.com

DEALING WITH THE WEATHER

The small town cafe was abuzz with the typical blend of ranchers and town folks having their morning coffee. Those out-of-towners who were unfortunate enough to get caught in the February blizzard were fixated on the 19-inch TV mounted in the upper corner of the room. The Weather Channel delivered the bad news again and again, but the visitors watched anyway, hoping that somehow the message would change and they could be on their way.

Schools closed. Freeways closed. A foot of snow on the ground and more coming. Subzero temperatures and 25 mph winds producing limited visibility and windchills low enough to freeze time. All the ingredients of a full-blown blizzard, the kind that kept sensible people at home.

I snuggled a little deeper into the booth and sipped my hot coffee as I listened to the drone of the weatherman, who seemed to derive perverse pleasure from repeatedly delivering the vile news. I was beginning to question the wisdom that had Bill Boyd,

Major Boddicker and me considering a coyote hunt on such an ominous morning. Bill and I exchanged glances across the table. I shook my head, and he nodded in agreement. I could picture every coyote in the country curled up into a tight little fur ball, nose to tail, just trying to ride out the storm. To venture out in such conditions would not only be foolhardy, but unproductive and even dangerous. But did we still have to try?

Bill and I babbled on about how any attempts to call coyotes under these conditions would be futile while Major sat quietly, stirring his coffee. Finally, apparently having heard enough, he looked up and with a twinkle in his eye delivered the words that encouraged me to smile and gather the gumption to collect my cap and gloves. "I seldom hunt with wimps, and never twice," he stated matter-of-factly. We were here to hunt coyotes and that's just what we were going to do, storm be damned!

It took everything Bill's pickup could muster to get us to the ranch that Bill had scouted weeks earli-

Weather Woes & What to Do

Wind: When winds hit 15 mph, predators head for heavy cover. All predators generally use whatever's there—creekbottoms, gorges, ravines, timber, cattails, high grass—to get out of the wind. Choose stands overlooking heavy cover and use lots of volume when calling in windy conditions. Any animals that are able to hear you should arrive in short order. Remain only 10 to 15 minutes on stands for foxes and coyotes, a little longer for cats. Space each stand one-quarter to one-half mile apart.

Cold & Heat: Hot coffee and frequent snacks help keep energy levels high and fight off cold and depressed attitudes. Dress in layers so that you can change with the temperatures. On hot steamy days, the cooler hours of the early morning and late evening produce the best results. Clear skies, blazing sun and 95-degree temperatures greatly reduce calling success.

Precipitation: Calling can be great on days with mist, light rain or light snow if you're prepared for it. Call near known food sources. Predators often "feed up" prior to storms. During most days of driving rains, and/or heavy snows and winds, it is generally a lot smarter to stay home and reload or handle fur. Predators are holed up and rarely come out.

er. He assured me that the ranch was crawling with coyotes, and I believed him, but I couldn't shake the feeling that we were just going through the motions. Visibility was near zero and the dim ranch roads were being consumed by deep pillow drifts of hard-packed snow. Still, we had to try, right?

The ranch was dissected by deep arroyos that ran north to south, and with the wind blowing from the northwest, they were our best bet for getting out of the wind. The driving snow would make long-range visibility tough, but if we could slip in and get out of the brunt of the wind maybe we had a chance of pulling a coyote up for a look-see. We would have to get close, though, because the sound of the call wasn't going to carry far.

The bitter wind found its way into every chink in my clothing as we walked out to make the first stand. I was chilled to the bone by the time I sat down just a hundred or so yards from the truck. Major and I slid just over the edge of a ridge. Bill lay prone on top between two arroyos about 20 yards over. Major did his best to get as much volume out of the Crit'R•Call Magnum as possible, sending the piteous wailings of a rabbit that was freezing to death deep into the crevices of the arroyo below us.

A couple of minutes into the stand, I looked over just in time to see Major shoulder his rifle and drop a coyote that was ascending the steep face of the ridge. He continued calling and about two minutes later I heard the muffled report of Bill's rifle. A coyote had appeared about 20 yards in front of him

When the going gets tough, the tough go hunting. Dressing in layers of warm clothing can help keep you in the field in sub-zero temperatures.

NOT FOR WIMPS

"Calling is not for wimps," Major Boddicker, owner of Rocky Mountain Wildlife Products, maker of the famed Crit'R•Call line of predator tubes, had told me that morning. He had also said, "Count on wind, cold, snow, rain, stickers, barbed wire punctures, flea bites, ant bites and sundry other assaults on one's body. But you do have some control over the weather if you dress properly, wear clothes tailored for the conditions and are versatile enough to change with them."

In cold weather, layer up and make sure you leave no exposed skin. Insulated coveralls help hold in body heat, and insulated boots, gloves, ski mask and a billed cap with ear flaps should help keep your extremities protected from the elements. Always bring a variety of clothes to match changing conditions, warm or cold. In warm climates, when it's likely to be cool in the morning but warm up as the day progresses, wear layers of camo clothing that you can easily remove as the temperature climbs, and still maintain full camo.

WHERE TO HUNT

When hunting in inclement weather, you might have to adjust your strategy to fit the situation. Cold weather, approaching or departing storm

circling the call to the downwind side, up out of the adjoining draw.

A double! And under conditions that would have kept most hunters at home in the recliner. I'd like to say that the unexpected success pushed aside all thoughts of the arctic temperatures, but I was freezing! We gathered up our dogs, made a mad dash to the truck and cranked up the heater.

We killed one more coyote that morning and another the next. Not great, but considering the conditions, it was the very best we could hope for. And I would have bet you the price of a prime high-country coyote that we weren't going to see so much as a flash of fur when I left the cafe that morning.

To this day, that trip remains one of the most memorable predator hunts I have ever been on, and the success we earned that day produced a standard that serves as a yardstick by which I measure all other hunts. It has given me the gumption to never say never when it comes to predator hunting. Truth be known, I've sat out many similar days, knowing full well that chances for success are diminished under such conditions. But every once in a while you've just got to push it to the limit.

During cold weather, predators are typically on the move hunting, trying to replace lost calories.

Predators can often be found near herds of deer and antelope or in brushy areas that hold smaller prey species like rabbits and rodents.

fronts, high wind, rain, even warm conditions can affect your success on any given day.

Three elements become increasingly important to all animals when the weather turns tough: food, water and shelter. For predators this might translate to deep draws with brushy cover where they can get out of the brunt of the wind and cold, and where they might find prey animals that are doing the same. Or in the case of extreme heat, it might be in a shaded area near a water source.

During a Colorado hunt, Major suggested that we hunt near a free-ranging herd of cattle on the ranch. He explained that it was calving season and coyotes would hang close to that food source—afterbirth, and even the newborn calves if they got the chance. Also, calf manure is high in protein for the first week or so and coyotes will feed on it as well. Analyze each situation and let the circumstances dictate your strategy and gear.

Predators will also be found near herds of deer and antelope, or in areas that hold small game such as old farm buildings, machinery and brush piles. Look for the types of cover that is home to rabbits, rodents and birds, and the critters that hunt them

will not be too far away.

In the East, I look to swamps and heavy stands of timber. Again, these areas offer shelter from the elements and are also the most productive places to hunt.

WINDY CONDITIONS

Predators are often more hesitant to respond in windy conditions because the efficiency of their senses is somewhat diminished. Not only is it more difficult for them to hear and respond to danger, their sense of smell is somewhat compromised by swirling winds. Predators are more apt to circle, so you must set up for that likelihood.

If you are hunting buddy-style, position the shooter as far as 100 yards downwind of the caller so he can take any cautiously approaching critters. If you're hunting alone, always make sure you have open shooting lanes downwind of your position to deal with circling customers.

Wind affects the distance at which predators can hear the call. This can be compensated for, somewhat, by using larger closed-reed calls that are capable of

Sure-Fire Tactics for Hunting Predators

In cold, windy conditions, use hills or ravines to shield yourself, and watch for predators circling to a downwind position.

producing considerable volume. Electronic callers are also helpful under windy conditions because they are capable of producing high volume.

When I call in windy conditions, I get into positions that overlook heavy cover such as creekbottoms, heavy brush or deep timber; then I call loudly. Sometimes a fox, coyote or bobcat will poke out of such cover to see what's going on. By sitting in an elevated position, you can sometimes take these animals that are probably not going to come to the call but will break cover just long enough to have a look around.

Weather greatly impacts calling success. And while hunting in heavy wind or rain is not advised, those times prior to or following a major storm system can be very productive. Some callers claim that calling is most productive when the barometer is falling rapidly.

Only by getting out in the field during all types of weather will you gain a better understanding of how the animals in various areas react to different conditions. Armed with that knowledge, you will better be able to decide the most productive hunting times.

Weather & Calling Success

Unpublished data compiled by Steve Allen, former furbearer biologist for the North Dakota Game and Fish Department, measured calling response rates for red foxes and coyotes, accounting for a number of variables. The Department polled more than 3,000 predator hunters about their calling response rates.

• **Time of Year:** The red fox response rate was higher in the winter months than in the autumn months, but coyote response was higher in the autumn and spring months. Similarly, red fox response rates were higher in colder temperatures, but coyote response rates were higher in warmer temperatures.

• **Snow Depth:** Red fox response rates were higher in relation to greater snow depths, but coyote response rates were higher in relation to less snow.

• **Barometric Pressure:** Red fox response rates were higher with a changing barometer, but coyote response rates were higher with a steady barometer.

• **Cloud Cover:** There was no significant difference in response rates for red foxes by percent of cloud cover: They were equally active under all conditions. But there was a higher response rate for coyotes by percent of cloud cover: The cloudier the sky, the more active the coyotes.

• **Precipitation and Wind:** There was no difference in the response rates for either species in relation to various levels of precipitation. Wind had a consistent negative impact on response rates for both red foxes and coyotes.

HUNTING THE MIXED BAG

F or a split second, I knew precisely what it feels like to be a mouse. The desert bobcat was closing the precious little ground between us at an alarming rate, her good eye (the second was milky white and useless) focused on the slight move-ment of my hand working the end of the closed-reed cottontail tube. She wasn't getting the big picture.

I panned the gun to meet the cat's advance just as Larry O. Gates let out a lip-squeak that brought the feline to an abrupt halt just 18 steps away. The

Bobcat

Coyote

Gray Fox

Red Fox

In most regions of the United States, two or more major predator species live in the same habitat, competing for the same food sources. That's good news for the equal-opportunity predator hunter.

Sure-Fire Tactics for Hunting Predators

The author carries out a bobcat, but success was as likely on coyotes and gray foxes considering the high desert terrain.

Model 788 barked as the 55-grainer left the barrel catbound. A millisecond later, the bobette was rugged out on the high-desert duff.

I was hunting the San Carlos Apache Indian Reservation east of Phoenix with friends Gerry Blair, Larry O. Gates and Gary "The Slammer" Hull. That expanse covers nearly 2 million acres of pure biodiversity: forests of plush ponderosa pine, alligator juniper, oak and pinyon pine; high desert dissected by brush-choked canyons; obtrusive rim rock. Predator heaven.

Larry and I had hiked in and set up just after high noon on the rim of a deep, brushy ravine that overlooked a creekbed far below. We were backed up against the sparse cover offered by a few scattered yuccas. It was the kind of setup that could produce any one of the predators that call the San Carlos home.

And while I had expected the stand to summon a coyote or two, even with the sun at its peak, I was

delighted and surprised to see the cat working the day shift. By the end of our three-day outing, we had put up a fine mixed bag of coyotes, bobcats and gray foxes.

EQUAL OPPORTUNITY HUNTER

Most regions of the United States have two or more major predator species living in the same habitat, competing for a community food source. In parts of the East, red and gray fox ranges overlap and are intertwined with those of the coyote, bobcat and raccoon. Out West, coyotes, gray foxes, bobcats and lions commonly shop the same friendly neighborhood grocery store for mammalian, feathered or crawly delectables.

This provides a delightful dilemma for the equal opportunity predator hunter. Consequently, every time the caller cuts loose on his favorite tube, he really has no way of knowing what might show up for dinner. The best way to deal with this situation is to expect the unexpected—and plan for the unplanned.

Gerry Blair and I had time to deliberate this topic while on the San Carlos. We hunted an entire day after a major storm without raising so much as a flea. That gave us plenty of time for discussion.

"Much of the time, a hunter sights in on a target species as he or she selects the calling country and the calling stand within that country," Gerry said in regard to hunting the mixed bag. "Even so, here in the West and in much of the East, an uncalled customer might respond. The Western hunter who targets coyotes in a greasewood flat, as an example, might draw a bobcat or gray fox from the mesquite-lined wash to his back. I take the time needed to evaluate the land and the response potential at each setup. Doing so causes me to perceive sneakers that might otherwise stay discreet."

THE PREDATOR EQUATION

If you recollect anything from eighth grade math (I had to look these up) you might remember terminology such as "common denominator" and "variables." By Webster's definition, common denominator refers to "… a number that can be evenly divided by all of the denominators of a set of fractions." In simpler terms, it refers to those things that have something in common. Variables are those things that are inconstant or different from other things.

By now you're probably wondering what the heck this has to do with predator hunting. Actually, these concepts apply well to hunting the mixed bag and illustrate the importance of analyzing each hunting situation for optimum results. Let me explain.

First, ask yourself what commonalties are shared by the predator species that inhabit the range where you hunt. Write these down. Come on, humor me.

The type of country hunted often dictates which predators will respond. But always be prepared for the unexpected guest.

Common Ground

First and foremost, predators are naturally going to share a common food source, such as rabbits, rodents, birds—maybe even deer or pronghorns. And don't forget plant matter and domestic fare. This can be applied to how they utilize their environment while on the prowl for food.

In addition to knowing what animals eat, Gerry says that knowing their habits and how they hunt their habitat to obtain food can provide a deadly advantage to the screamer. "Knowing that a bobcat is

Red foxes favor open terrain where they can see and smell danger from a safe distance.

often a sneak," he explains, "one that prefers the safety of cover, can provide an insight into its approach. Those new to the sport (even some not so new) become so focused on calling and killing a red fox, for instance, that they do not evaluate the land at the stand. Their setup might be effective against the red, which they expect to respond, but less effective against the coyote, bobcat or raccoon that might make a surprise visit."

What other similarities come to mind? Predators typically have access to only the same sources of water, the same cover, the same travel routes and so on. You get the picture. These are all examples of the things that the predators in your area hold in common. It is the reason they live there and how they survive.

Differences

Now let's have a look at the variables.

Animal hunting techniques might vary. Some predators work the night shift while others commonly hunt during daylight hours. Coyotes prefer open spaces in the West, while cats and gray foxes are more likely to work heavy cover. In the East, it is common for coyotes to frequent the big timber while red foxes hunt the open farm fields and pastures.

And how do they hunt? A feline, being a creeper, might take a half hour or more to make its way to the call, while coyotes and gray foxes, often chargers, are more likely to show within the first few minutes of the call.

Then there's the difference in how they use their sensory systems. Felines, for example, are visual hunters, using their keen eyesight to detect and stalk their prey, while canines depend primarily on their noses.

Now that you've analyzed the commonalties and differences between the predators that you hunt, how can you apply this knowledge to the hunting situation?

Take a look at the list you've just compiled and an equation should emerge that will allow you to take better advantage of hunting a multi-species area. Let's apply this information to gun selection, stand selection and calling techniques to get you started.

Hunting brush-choked ravines (right), you will likely attract bobcats and gray foxes. Some enterprising hunters (below), carry both a shotgun and a rifle to each stand so that they are better prepared for any scenario.

GUN SELECTION

Using the common denominator/variables equation, you will quickly note that no particular gun will be the right choice under all conditions. A caliber that will rug out a 130-pound desert lion, say .22-250 Rem. up, will kill a 10-pound gray fox occupying the same territory a whole lot deader than need be. And that same long-range rifle topped with a high-power scope will not serve you well in the brushy cover of the East or the desert tangles or woody canyons of the West.

Some compromise must be made in regard to sure-kill potential and fur recovery as well as to long- vs. short-range shot opportunities.

Sure-Fire Tactics for Hunting Predators

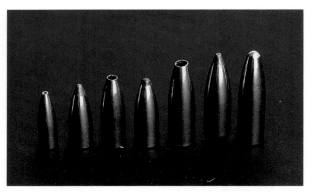

Predator hunters have a wide array of bullet configurations and weights to choose from to balance the needs of killing the animal cleanly and preserving its valuable fur.

Let's look at some of the fur guns that would apply to some of the predators that you might encounter, and see if we can spot any common denominators.

In the West, opportunity for the long shot—which may be your only shot—exists. Your choice of firearms should reflect this possibility. Calibers such as the .22-250 Rem., .25-06 Rem. and .243 Win. immediately come to mind. These and other like calibers will reach out and touch predators at a considerable distance and handle the largest Western canines and felines. But you might sacrifice some fur as you step up muscle to obtain long-range accuracy.

Like most Western callers, Gerry Blair packs two guns—a rifle and a shotgun—in the pickup. He lets the stand dictate which gun stays behind. "I call pretty much the same for the big three: coyotes, foxes and bobcats," he says. "If I am teamed up, I might carry a shotgun in close country, asking that my partner carry a rifle, or vice versa. When solo calling, I almost always carry a rifle of a caliber stout enough to whack the bashful bobcat or the cougar that might hang up a couple of football fields away."

In the East, where human occupancy and tight terrain is common, long-range shooting opportunities are somewhat diminished and the above-mentioned calibers often supply more horsepower than is necessary, especially in fox country. Eastern hunters might consider some of the small-but-deadly calibers such as

the .17 Rem., the .22 Hornet, .222 Rem. or .223 Rem. Keep in mind, however, that the Eastern coyote is a large and sturdy animal which might require more killing than a 10-pound fox. If you are hunting in proven coyote country, your gun choice should provide the foot-pounds of energy needed to topple a 50-pound-plus dog.

The rule of thumb is to use a caliber that will be hefty enough for the largest predator that you might encounter, but will keep fur damage minimal on the smallest. Of course there is no such magic cure-all caliber, so the best you can hope for is a caliber and gun setup that falls somewhere in the middle. As a general guideline, the .22-250 Rem. is considered a good all-around fur gun in the West and the .223 Rem. serves as a good Eastern fur-getter.

Do not discount the value of a shotgun in tight country or when working the night shift. In heavy cover, where action is likely to be fast and fierce, a scattergun loaded with buckshot or BBs is often your

The rule of thumb is to use a caliber that will be hefty enough to handle the largest predator that you might encounter, and that will minimally damage the smallest.

best choice. This is a lethal fur-taker at close range, and pelt damage is typically minimal. Many Eastern hunters prefer to use shotguns at night for safety considerations.

STAND SELECTION

When hunting areas where two or more predatory species might be present, take the time to analyze your stand selection thoroughly. On the San Carlos, the terrain transitioned from open range to brush-choked canyons to obtrusive rimrock. And animal sign was a constant reminder that lions, bobcats, gray foxes and coyotes were all using the diverse landscape with varying degrees of regularity. We found that setting up near large open expanses usually gave up coyotes, while the brushy canyons and rimrock were where the lions, bobcats and gray foxes hung out.

When I hunt the East, I typically set up in transition zones from heavy cover to some type of opening. Most critters like to hug the heavy cover before committing to the call and breaking out into the open.

Know what each animal prefers in respect to home range and its own hunting technique, and set up accordingly. In areas where cats are as likely to come to the call as canines, you must prepare for critters working the wind as well as those scanning the landscape for movement.

There are a number of ways you can work the wind in your favor. Contrary to what you've often heard or read, the wind doesn't always have to be in your face, even though it's usually the best option. A wise and experienced caller once told me, "If coyotes always worked into the wind, they'd all be in California."

If the lay of the land allows, it is best to set up with the wind in your face overlooking the areas from which you expect your company to arrive. But you must also account for the fact that some animals will try to get in behind you or from the side. Use a natural barrier such as a water source or some other obstruction to prevent them from circling to your position.

Set up similarly in a crosswind. If the animal approaches downwind in your shooting lane, it will not pick up on your scent until it's too late. If the wind is blowing from right to left, I like to keep an

Hunting bobcats requires that you set up in some pretty tough terrain. Your challenges are to find the cover that these cats prefer, and also to find shooting lanes so that you can see a cat approach and make a good shot.

open shooting lane to my left to pick up on anything that might be circling downwind. I find that setting up in a crosswind works well when the wind is blowing at a pretty good clip.

If I'm hunting a wide open area with good visibility, I sometimes set up about two-thirds the way up a hill and call downwind. The predators will generally work from one side or the other to the downwind position trying to pick up on my scent. A high-powered rifle on a steady rest will usually pick up these predators before they detect you.

CALLING TECHNIQUES

You've no doubt heard that canines come more quickly to the call than do cats. And the majority of the time this is true. But not all predators subscribe to these or any set of rules. My San Carlos cat, for example, appeared only 10 minutes into the scream, and at high noon to boot. The reason ... who knows?

Most Western callers rarely spend more than 15 to 20 minutes at a stand where coyotes are expected and rarely exceed 30 to 40 minutes when bobcats and lions are the called critters. Eastern callers, because of the heavier cover and tighter terrain, should extend those parameters a bit. In fact, I know a successful caller in Vermont who tells me he sits on each stand no less than 45 minutes and has customers sneak in well past the time when most callers would have packed it in. If heavy cover is typical where you hunt, you can expect predators to use that cover to put the sneak on your position.

Western hunters generally stay on a stand 15 to 20 minutes where coyotes are expected and stretch that to 30 minutes or more where bobcats or mountain lions might show.

If you're hunting the mixed bag, the common denominators must be considered when determining how long to sit it out. Those commonalties will include wind direction and velocity, cover, the type of predator you're calling to and so on. Here are a few rules of thumb that can serve as guidelines.

- If there is the likelihood that a cat or lion might make an appearance, extend your stay at the stand. Sit no less than 30 minutes for bobcats and consider sticking it out for an hour if you have your sights set on a lion.

- In heavy wind, your sound will not carry as well and you can typically shorten your stay at the stand as well as the distance between them. Any predator that hears you and is inclined to come is probably in close proximity and will arrive at your location in short order. Increase volume in windy conditions; an electronic caller is a good choice.

- If you are hunting in heavy cover, give the predator more time to get to you. It will no doubt use the available cover to sneak to your position, slowing its advance.

- Knowing some predators are more timid than others, I usually start my calling session with very little volume and build it up. In country where I expect red foxes to show, for example, I start with very little volume and call infrequently. If nothing shows within the first 10 minutes or so, I begin increasing the volume, hoping to reach out to a fox or coyote that might be hanging up some distance away.

Whether you're hunting the expansive West, the woodlands of the East, Midwestern farmlands or the prairie grasslands, knowing your quarry well and knowing how they use their terrain will help you solve the predator hunting puzzle. And take a tip from your eighth grade math teacher: Use common denominators and variables to take the best advantage of the opportunities of the mixed bag. 'Cause you never know who just might show up for dinner.

SCOUTING

Probably no other element of hunting is more critical than scouting. Knowing animal travel patterns and densities and the lay of the land can ensure that you work the most fruitful areas and avoid those that are unproductive. Trappers seek out rich fur pockets that will produce year after year and you can do the same in your predator hunting. Find those elements that provide the creature comforts that predators seek out—food, water and shelter. Devise a plan that will put you in contact with as many animals as possible.

MAPPING YOUR ROUTE

Whether you're contemplating an extensive out-of-state predator hunting venture, or simply expanding your local hunting haunts, you need a plan. It's not enough to zigzag helter-skelter across the countryside hoping to discover rich fur pockets. The best-laid plans typically yield the best results.

Always work from the general to the specific when mapping out your hunting scheme. Begin by making general observations and then fine-tune to the specific. Much of your initial work can be done without leaving the comfort of your home. Obtain maps of the areas you will hunt. These could be state road maps if you're planning an extensive hunt, or a county road map if you're hunting close to home. Also obtain Forest Service, BLM and public hunting ground maps that detail public lands where hunting is allowed.

Study the riparian (water) and topographic qualities of the landscape, as well as how roadways intersect probable predator travelways. This will give you a feel for the overall quality of the property you choose to hunt.

Getting down to the nitty-gritty will require a trip afield, locating specific stand locations and plotting the most cost- and time-effective course of action.

Land generally falls into two categories: private and public. If you are considering hunting on public land, contact the wildlife agency of the state you plan to hunt. They can provide detailed license information, as well as information regarding public land and the relative abundance of predators. Many have maps of wildlife management areas, and guides to public and private camping facilities.

If you plan to hunt on private property, obtain county plat maps for areas where you will concentrate your efforts. These are available from most county courthouses. By using a plat book in conjunction with other maps, you can determine where public land abuts private land and also obtain the names of property owners. I have also purchased aerial photographs, available from some state forestry services, to help make actual stand selections without setting foot on the property.

Scout and select good stand locations to maximize your time afield.

GETTING THE LOWDOWN

Landowners can be a valuable source of information. And if you're planning to hunt private land, you will be talking to a lot of ranchers and farmers. They know their properties intimately and can tell you when and where they've seen predators throughout the year. Don't be afraid to ask to hunt; most landowners aren't protective of predators like

they are their deer, turkeys or gamebirds. In fact, you might be welcomed with open arms.

The rural mail carrier or delivery service driver can also provide useful information. These people spend a considerable amount of time on rural roads and observe wildlife as they travel the countryside. They know who lives where and what property they own. County extension agents or conservation officers might provide you with names of livestock producers who are having problems with foxes or coyotes raiding their poultry.

Local fur buyers usually know what areas are fur producers and how much hunting and trapping pressure they receive. If you have friends who bowhunt, pick their brains about the predators they see while on stand early in the fall. Many spend considerable time in treestands and observe predators as they make their evening and morning rounds. Some will share this information as long as it doesn't jeopardize their chance at a deer.

STAND SELECTION

Scouting out and selecting good stand locations prior to the hunt will ensure efficient use of your time afield. To be successful, you need to determine your quarry's food sources and how it uses its habitat.

And you must continue to scout your hunting areas throughout the season. Food and water sources and available cover can change with the seasons, and predator travel patterns will mirror those changes.

Landowners can give you the lowdown on where you might find predators hanging out.

I like to drive around an area taking general notes regarding the lay of the land and how heavy cover meets open areas. If I'm hunting coyote country, I might try a little howling to determine population densities and travel patterns.

Next, I select specific stand locations that I can return to, and then mark them on a map or write down their locations for later reference. They won't all turn out to be gems, but it gives me a place to start.

Have a rough travel route laid out before you leave your truck, taking into consideration the direction and velocity of the wind, the amount of time you have, and generally what you want to accomplish in the time you have.

I always try to have my first three stand locations picked out, keeping them relatively close together. The first stands after daybreak are often the most productive, and I don't want to waste time driving around the countryside trying to decide where to set up.

In the West, I might look for heavy cover that breaks into more open country. Grassy draws, dry washes and foothills all provide transition zones from one type of terrain into another. Predators hunt these "edges," which can be very productive.

In the East, farmers often put up hay in large, round bales and leave them in the field until needed. These offer excellent setups in open farm country where cover is scarce.

Old farm machinery left to the elements often have weeds and brush growing in and around them. These provide good cover and sometimes offer a rest from which to shoot. Abandoned farm buildings, grown up fencerows, dozer piles, trash piles ... any bit of cover can make for a good place to set up.

Some farmland is split by railroad right-of-ways or by large drainage ditches. This is often the only cover available for miles; predators and prey alike are attracted to these areas, as you should be.

As you hike around on properties, be in constant search of tracks and scat that indicate where predators are traveling, as well as what they are hunting and what they are eating.

To have productive predator hunts, you need the efficiency that comes from intensive planning and scouting. It isn't enough to run around the countryside haphazardly making stand after stand. Efficiency breeds positive results, and preparing for your hunt can help achieve the biggest bang for your dollar.

Advanced scouting translates into success on the stand. Knowing predator traveling and hunting patterns can put you sure-kill close.

LOCATION, LOCATION, LOCATION

Allen Moeller eased the truck to the edge of the dim road and killed the diesel engine. It gave a slight shudder and quietly expired. He rolled down his window and a cool breeze permeated the cab. I snuggled a little deeper into the comfort of the bench seat and sipped my lukewarm coffee.

We sat silently, listening to a pair of song dogs exchange pleasantries a mile or more to the north. Allen looked over and gave me a nod. We knew the routine, even though we had never hunted together. Quietly exiting the truck, we grabbed our gear and melted into the predawn murk.

The first stand of the morning is magical. The air is crisp and clear, senses are keen and anticipation is high. I could hear the subtle changing of the guard as I quietly followed in Allen's footsteps. Day critters, shaking off a night's restless sleep, began foraging for food, adding their voices to the morning choir. Slowly, dawn replaced night.

Coyotes on the trail-end of their nightly patrol were still on the hunt. Those unsuccessful during the night were anxious to fill their bellies before the morning sun turned the Texas landscape steamy hot. I settled into my stand, my back against a small tree, while Allen fiddled with the electronic caller. Soon the sounds of a desperate rabbit pierced the still morning air. I pulled my knees up close to my chest and readied my rifle.

The first stand was a no-show, as were the two stands that followed. Determined to do better, Allen and I crouched low as we topped a rimrock ridge, trying not to skyline ourselves as we worked our way to the next stand.

Our elevated position, two-thirds the way up a semi-steep ridge, gave us a panoramic view of the valley below. We would be able to see coyotes approaching from a half mile or more. Prepared for that likely event, I was toting my favorite coyote gun, my .243 Win.

Not three minutes into the next stand, a coyote charged the call directly below us, less than 30 yards out, catching us completely off guard. So much for the best laid plans.

Creatures of habit, coyotes utilize the same areas year after year. Get to know where these fur pockets are and you'll find old Wily.

I shouldered the rifle, knowing I would need a bunch of luck to turn our dogless day around. Allen, being the gracious host, held his 12 gauge at bay while I frantically panned hard to the left.

The coyote, in the meantime, recognized its poor judgment and switched ends, heading for home and Mother.

Too late. I caught a flash of dusty brown fur in the scope, swung on the shoulder and lit the fire. I had failed to adjust for the sharp angle and the bullet hit a little high, but it was close enough in this case—doubly so because Allen, unable to contain his enthusiasm any longer, had squeezed the trigger in pure syn-chronism. The coyote hit the

You have to hunt predators where they are; the ability to consistently select productive stand locations is crucial to success.

turf with gusto—double dead.

Allen and I slapped each other on the back, took the mandatory handful of photos and hauled the coyote to the truck. That coyote turned our luck around, and a couple of stands later we had our second dog.

FAMILIARITY EQUALS GOOD LOCATIONS EQUALS SUCCESS

One of the reasons we were successful that morning is that Allen was familiar with the prop-erty on which we were hunting. We didn't have to waste a lot of time scouting and we weren't running helter-skelter around the ranch trying to determine where the coyotes were hanging out.

You have to hunt predators where they are, and the ability to consistently select productive

Sure-Fire Tactics for Hunting Predators

In the West, predators seek out tough cover where they can bed down or hunt for prey.

stand locations is a crucial basic element of predator hunting that separates good callers from the best.

Montana Animal Damage Control (ADC) trapper John Graham says that he likes to size up the country before he ever sets foot on it, to determine where the best fur pockets are and how to get to them. While this certainly includes getting out and scouting on foot, John says you can learn a lot by driving around the boundaries of the property and assessing it as a whole.

"I try to pinpoint the three or four best places on the ranch where I think coyotes, foxes or bobcats will be spending the majority of their time," he told me on a late January hunt. "These are generally natural funnels, like a travel way, a road intersection, where a draw meets a river, or where a wheat field backs up against heavy cover."

"Basically, I look for rough cover, like brushy creekbeds, where predators might be bedded down or hunting for rabbits and mice. The more you hunt, the more you get a feel for the places where predators live rather than just travel through. To be consistently successful you have to identify these core areas. Typically, these places are similar from ranch to ranch and you're able to identify them once you know what you're looking for."

DETAILS OF A GOOD LOCATION

John says that the actual setup is very important too. "You don't want too many hills up close in front of you if you can help it. Predators will hang up or go around a hill right in front of you, out of

sight as they circle your setup," he says. "I like to get into a position where I have a good view of at least 50 or 100 yards all around me. You don't want any places where incoming predators are hidden from your view."

Selecting the exact location of your setups can depend on a number of variables. One of the most important variables has to do with how predators use the features of their habitat.

As an example, the North Dakota study I referred to earlier concluded that red fox response rates declined the farther hunters set up from roads or occupied houses, but coyote response rates increased when the hunter selected calling stands farther from roads or occupied houses. This is a valuable piece of information if you're targeting one of the two species in an area where they both exist.

Hunters wanting to maximize red fox response rates should keep most of their calling effort within one-half to one mile of graded roads or occupied houses and farms; however, hunters wanting to maximize coyote response rates should concentrate their efforts farther than one-half mile from roads and occupied houses and farms. This pattern probably occurs because of differences in home range spacing by the two species. Earlier home-range/territory studies in North Dakota utilizing radio telemetry demonstrated that coyotes selected the larger, more remote areas for themselves and left red fox areas closer to roads and houses.

Where red foxes occupy the same territory as coyotes, they can often be found closer to roads or farm buildings.

SETTING UP

Once you're on location you are halfway home. If you've done a good job of scouting and made sound decisions in selecting your stand locations, there is a good chance that you're within earshot of the predators you are attempting to call. The next steps are critical to success. Pure and simple, the primary objective of calling predators is to get the animal close enough to make a lethal shot.

The best general advice I can offer is to let the terrain dictate the nature of the setup. When I walk into an area for a setup, I run through a mental checklist that will dictate exactly where I sit, how I call, how long I stay and so on. Here's what to consider:

VISIBILITY

It is imperative that you have good visibility. When you walk into a stand, you must look for the precise spot that offers you the greatest visual advantage. That might mean an elevated position, cover to break your outline, wind and sun advantage. Settle for nothing less. Look at it this way. The wily coyote or sneaky bobcat you call up will do the same. That predator, your prey, will use every available piece of cover, every high or low blemish in the terrain, every trick in the book to put a sneak on your location.

SPACING

The distance you travel between stands is determined by what kinds of animals you are hunting, the weather, the terrain and a host of other factors. In open terrain, where sound carries great distances, you might want to put a mile or more between stands to ensure that you are calling to a fresh pair of ears or any ears at all.

In hilly or brushy country, where vegetation and breaks in the topography cut the distance that sound will travel, you might need only move one-quarter mile between setups. If I'm hunting in canyon country, I might call down several different deep draws from a single ridgetop.

Wind will also knock the punch out of calls. On windy days, your sound will not carry nearly as far, and you can keep your stands at closer intervals, even in open country.

Sure-Fire Tactics for Hunting Predators

WIND & SUN

Ideally, you would always have the wind in your face and the sun at your back when on stand, but of course this is not always possible. So try to obtain a compromise. I always consider the wind first, and will sacrifice the position of the sun to get favorable wind direction. But remember, if you can get the sun to your back it makes it much more difficult for approaching predators to pick you up and, even better, makes it easier for you to see them.

Where visibility is good, sitting provides you with a steady rest and allows you to blend in with the environment.

SIT OR STAND

I let the terrain dictate whether I sit or stand. If the cover is just too thick to allow good visibility while sitting, I'll try to stand next to a tree, bush, boulder or other large object to break up my silhouette. This is often the case when hunting brushy riverbottoms or dry washes with a shotgun. The predators take advantage of the heavy cover for hunting too and to escape danger. They might show up without a moment's notice and, if you're standing, you might have a better chance of getting the drop on them with your scattergun.

CREATURE COMFORTS

Knowing full well that I'm going to have to be as still as a rock and quiet as a mouse for 15 minutes or more, I go out of my way to select setups that offer as much comfort as possible. And I generally carry a small cushion to soften the roost and protect my butt from those pokey plants while I hide in waiting. If you're hunting in snow, a cushion keeps your bottom warm and dry as the snow melts underneath you.

Look for a solid object to back up against. This helps alleviate fatigue and also helps break up your outline. Backing into a snowbank, tree, fencepost, hay bale or the like will make your stay at a stand more pleasant.

If you can find a slightly elevated throne, so much the better. This will allow for your feet to be below your butt, permitting a free flow of blood. There's nothing worse than having your feet fall asleep while at the stand.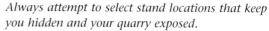

Always attempt to select stand locations that keep you hidden and your quarry exposed.

Three Strategies for Success

Consistent predator hunting success isn't happenstance. It is the result of thoughtful planning, intensive scouting, insight into animal behavior and the culmination of years of field experience.

Without exception, the best predator callers I have met are those who do it for a living. Animal Damage Control (ADC) agents, who work for state and federal wildlife and agricultural agencies, cattle and sheep associations or private farms and ranches, take predator calling to a higher level. Their jobs demand it.

When the casual predator hunter goes afield, he does not concern himself with the hard cases—those animals that have seen and heard it all before. He is more interested in impressing the uneducated, the uninformed—generally, the young-of-year.

But ADC professionals must often target individual nuisance animals. You and I can walk away if the going gets tough. These gentlemen do not have that option. This is their job. They must dig deep into their bag of tricks and come up with a twist on a rudimentary technique that will fool the unfoolable and trick the trickster. They must think like a predator ... become a predator.

By learning more about coyote behavior, you will be better equipped to achieve consistent results.

So on the rare occasion when one of these veterans shares a few golden nuggets of wisdom, I turn an attentive ear and take mental notes. On several occasions I've hunted with Scott Huber, an ADC agent for the South Dakota Division of Wildlife. On a prairie hunt he offered the following strategies basic to coyote hunting mastery.

Don't Call to Danger

Trying to call coyotes toward a source of danger might limit your success. Many times people will drive down a road, stop and walk in a little way from their vehicle to make a stand. There's a good chance that the coyotes in that area have been shot at from the road and view it as a source of danger.

But instead of realizing what's going on, that hunter blames himself or becomes discouraged because he thinks he is doing something wrong. In this case, it would be better to venture deeper into Wily's backyard, to get away from the road and in sections where he's not used to hearing a predator call. Calling him away from the perceived danger just might be the ticket.

Don't Call to Coyotes That Aren't There

Just because an area looks good doesn't mean coyotes are using every square inch of it. The hunter must determine through scouting, talking to landowners and maybe even using a siren or howler, if and where the coyotes are spending the majority of their time.

The flip side of this strategy is that just because coyotes don't respond to the call doesn't mean they aren't there. Sometimes coyotes will hold up and not come in because they have a belly full of food and aren't hungry. Or they might be traveling to a food source in one direction while you're trying to pull them in another. Again, if you've done your homework, you know if there are coyotes in the area, whether they come to the call or not. You might just have to come back another time, or try calling from another location.

Don't Try to Pull Them Too Far

If coyotes will answer your howls but they won't come in, they simply might be too far away. When this happens, you are going to have to move toward them. Use available cover to shave off the distance between you and the coyotes. Work in closer, set up and try calling again. They might come in silently, so be prepared for action.

Chapter Five

THE BIG FOUR

No matter where you reside, you can take comfort in knowing that you have at least one, and probably most, of the "Big Four" hanging out in your backyard. Coyotes, red foxes, gray foxes and bobcats all live in relative abundance across the North American continent. And while some of these species are regionally more plentiful than others, most predator hunters can go afield in search of the mixed bag.

Western hunters, in particular, are equal opportunity predator callers. In many regions of the Southwest, for example, they might call up any one of these species during a single outing. Most often, however, the type of terrain hunted will determine the sort of animal that responds. Bobcats and gray foxes, in Texas, might hang out in brushy draws and rimrock canyons, while coyotes and red foxes live and hunt in the massive plains and rolling hills.

Eastern hunters, too, can experience a multi-species predator hunt. For example, hunters who chase red foxes with regularity have experienced the arrival of coyotes in many of their favorite areas, as the animal has pushed the eastern boundaries of its range in recent decades. Bobcats and gray foxes fill niches in habitat that the coyote finds less palatable.

While previous chapters have offered tips and techniques utilized by the multi-species predator hunter, it's now time to have a closer look at the idiosyncrasies and individual characteristics of each of the major predators we hunt—how they differ from each other and how we can use that knowledge to better target each one.

By gaining a better understanding of what makes each of these animals tick, you will take an important step forward in the progression from a casual predator hunter to a master of the game—one who's better prepared to match wits with the most wary of adversaries.

HUNTING COYOTES

*I*t is difficult to mention the word coyote without adding the adjective that invariably precedes it … wily. And those predator hunters who have matched wits with this cunning adversary know that the coyote is wily to the Nth degree.

"Opportunistic" best describes the coyote's eating habits, if not its lifestyle. Both a scavenger and predator, its diet consists of small animals and birds, livestock, deer, carrion, reptiles, amphibians, insects and many plant species. You name it, the coyote eats it.

This is one reason coyotes have been able to exist in such a variety of habitats, and is one of the keys to its survival in an environment constantly altered by man. In fact, the coyote has not only survived, but flourished.

Once a predominantly Western predator, the coyote has expanded its range eastward in recent decades and now occupies most of North America.

An agricultural boom in the mid- to late-1800s destroyed habitat needed to sustain many big game species, which decreased wolves' available food sources. That, coupled with the relentless persecution of remaining wolves, led to its extirpation throughout most of its traditional range. The removal of wolves paved the way for the coyote's highly successful migration eastward. By the early 1900s, the coyote had gained a firm foothold in most Eastern states and Canadian provinces.

In the West, coyotes are likely to be found wherever the habitat provides food, water and shelter for the prey animals they seek. Brushy draws, riverbeds, grassy plains, high deserts and deep canyons make up much of their home range. In the East, coyotes prefer forests, woodland edges, swamp edges and areas containing thickets of brush or tall vegetation. Farmland makes decent coyote country too nowadays.

Coyotes are very social and territorial animals that use complex vocalizations to communicate and establish territories and dominance. Their social system is built upon a strict hierarchy in which members of the society hold dominant or submissive positions. Assertive males passionately guard their territories, and intruders are severely dealt with.

While coyotes do not mate for life in most cases,

Extremely social animals, coyotes communicate through complex vocalizations and body language.

they might choose the same partner several years in a row. Western coyotes commonly hunt in pairs, while it has been found that Eastern coyotes are more apt to hunt in small packs.

Of the "Big Four," coyotes are generally the most sought-after predator in most regions east and west. Their inherent wily nature and paranoid disposition make them challenging and sometimes frustrating to hunt.

Public land is often overlooked by fur hunters but, truth be known, good hunting can often be found on these underutilized properties. In the West, this might mean Bureau of Land Management holdings, U.S. Forest Service and State Trust lands, or huge Indian reservations. In the East, Wildlife Management Areas, Conservation Reserve Program lands, paper company landholdings and county, state and federal forest lands all provide good coyote hunting opportunities.

Coyotes, east and west, are often shunned by farmers and ranchers, and access to prime private property is relatively easy to obtain for the purpose of hunting these "despicable" critters. By knocking on a few doors or contacting local agricultural extension agents or conservation officers, you might be able to

obtain the names of landowners who might have had trouble with coyotes in the past—or have it now—and would willingly give you passage to their land.

Like the white-tailed deer, the coyote has demonstrated its ability to adapt to man's encroachment upon its domain. Its intelligence and cunning have earned it both the admiration of those who hunt and trap it, and the scorn of ranchers and farmers.

Like the coyote or not, it is here to stay.

I once heard it said that if we ever have a nuclear war only cockroaches and coyotes will survive. I don't know about cockroaches, but I have no doubt that coyotes would somehow thrive and prosper.

GEARING UP FOR COYOTES

Guns & Accessories

Any of the .22 centerfire calibers is a good choice for coyotes. Hunters who operate in the open expanses of the West generally prefer the flat-shooting .22-250 Rem., .25-06 Rem., .243 Win. and similar calibers. Eastern hunters, who often operate in tighter terrain and in more populated areas, generally opt for lighter calibers such as the .223 Rem., .222 Rem. Mag.,

.220 Swift or even the mighty-but-tiny .17 Rem. The .22 Win. Mag. rimfire, popular among many fox hunters, is generally too light for coyotes and should be avoided.

Most serious hunters prefer bolt-action rifles for their inherent accuracy, dependability and their capacity to deliver relatively quick follow-up shots. Bolt actions can handle more abuse than pumps, levers and autoloaders, and hunters who use them in the adverse conditions innate to predator calling appreciate their durability. The bolt action will simply handle more bumping, bruising and bad weather than other actions and keep on performing.

For coyotes, I like the plastic-tipped bullets such as Nosler's Ballistic tip loaded in factory ammo produced by Federal, Remington, Weatherby and Winchester; they're accurate and effective.

The importance of having a solid shooting platform is paramount to predator hunting. Bipods and shooting sticks should be standard equipment and carried at all times. Coyotes often hold

Any of the .22 caliber centerfire bullets (above) available to hunters will anchor even the meanest coyote.

up at 200 to 300 yards and a steady rest is needed for these long, difficult shots. I prefer to use shooting sticks because I can quickly kick them out of the way and shoot offhand if I get surprised by a hard-charging coyote.

Fixed-power scopes in the 6X to 8X range work best for coyotes. Many hunters believe that using a fixed-power scope helps them determine distance to their target because they are always using the same magnification.

Shotguns are the best choice when hunting in tight cover or at night. Copper-plated BBs or No. 4 buckshot in 3-inch 12 gauge or 3½-inch 10 gauge loads will anchor even the toughest coyotes out to 40 yards. Special-purpose pump-action or autoloading guns (with camo or flat-black finishes developed for turkey hunters) are perfect for predator hunting.

These guns also have relatively short barrels—usually 22 or 24 inches—for quick handling.

Calls

Either open-reed or closed-reed calls—those that imitate the sounds of cottontails, snowshoe hares or jackrabbits in distress—will work well for coyotes. Coyotes are not as sensitive to volume as many other predators, and calls that put out good volume will sometimes draw coyotes from a half mile or more away.

While closed-reed calls are easier to use, open-reed calls are capable of producing a wide variety of sounds and are favored by most callers. I do a considerable amount of walking when I'm hunting coyotes, and for that reason I generally prefer to use hand calls over electronic callers. Hand calls are portable, inexpensive, easy to use and dependable; and if you carry several, like I do, you have a variety of sounds at your disposal.

Shotguns are a good choice for coyotes in the East where cover is often tight. Buckshot or BBs do a dandy job out to 40 yards or so.

Most hunters carry a variety of hand calls that produce different pitches and volumes to fit the occasion.

Electronic calls are a good option when you need extra volume—such as on windy days, or when you are calling in an area that has been worked over by other hunters. Tapes provide a variety of sounds that will sometimes appeal to otherwise call-shy coyotes. My favorite "switch-up" tape for coyotes is the sound of a gray fox in distress. This often works wonders when more typical rabbit-in-distress sounds fail.

A howler makes a good change-up to the rabbit-in-distress sounds that most hunters use. Howlers are particularly effective during the January/February mating season when coyotes are claiming and defending their territories. Howlers are also effective for locating coyotes.

STRATEGIES FOR HUNTING COYOTES

Stand Selection

Above all, do your best to make sure you have good visibility in all directions. Try not to leave any blind spots.

Coyotes will typically try to circle downwind of your position and use any available cover, even slight breaks in the terrain, when approaching the call. An elevated stand will give you better visibility and your sound will carry much

Good visibility is paramount to successful coyote calling. Sit up high if you can, with the wind blowing into or across your face.

farther, but always select a shelf below the skyline. Break your outline with brush, a tree, a yucca, a cedar bush, a rock or any other available cover. You can get away with some movement as long as your outline is somewhat broken up.

Set up with the wind blowing into or across your face. Optimally, the sun should be at your back. Again, make sure you have an open shooting lane downwind of your position, so you have a chance at those sneaky, circling coyotes.

Calling Sequence

Regarding how often you should get on the tube or how much volume to use, there seem to be as many variations as there are hunters. I'm not as concerned with volume when calling coyotes as I am with the smaller predators, but never begin a calling sequence at full volume. I generally blow the tube or play the tape for about 20 to 30 seconds and then remain quiet for about a minute. I rarely stay at the stand for more than 15 minutes when targeting coyotes. I have found that most show within the first 10 minutes, and many within the first minute or two where populations are dense.

Night Hunting

Where legal, night hunting for coyotes can be fun and productive. Coyotes are generally more bold under the cover of darkness and respond aggressively to the call. Most of the same rules apply to hunts during the night as during the day in regard to stand selection and calling techniques.

Use an artificial light with an amber or red lens cover to scan for the reflective eyes of your quarry. When hunting where there is snow cover, you can use the light of the moon to identify your target. I generally hunt with a shotgun when hunting by the light of the moon; I want my target close

The Big Four

so that I can make positive identification before I pull the trigger.

Dealing with Doubles

Coyotes often hunt in pairs and it's not unusual to have more than one show up at a stand, sometimes coming from different directions. How you handle these situations will often determine whether you leave with one, two or even no coyotes. If you're hunting alone, always take the coyote that presents the best shot first, hopefully the closer of the two. Only when you have him anchored should you turn your attention to the second.

If you are hunting with a partner, an imaginary line should divide your shooting lanes. If you are positioned to your buddy's right, you should take all coyotes to the right of that imaginary line.

Always try for a standing shot on the first coyote. When a pair of coyotes charges in, I usually bark loudly when they get inside 100 yards. This will usually cause them to momentarily stop and survey the situation. Again— always take the easiest shot first, and make sure you have one coyote down before you turn your attention to the departing song dog.

When coyotes show up in pairs, take the easy shot first and then get back on the call to freeze the other animal in its tracks.

Coyote Profile

Coyotes can weigh as much as 40 pounds—even more in their Eastern range. That puts them high on the predator food chain in most locales.

The coyote is midway in size between a fox and a wolf. An adult male is about 44 to 52 inches long, including its 14-inch tail, and weighs, on average, from 25 to 42 pounds. Female coyotes are generally one-fifth smaller in size and weight than males.

Long, thin legs, a tapered muzzle and rather large, pointed ears characterize this member of the canine family. The coyote's black-tipped bushy tail, which comprises about a third of the body length, is carried below the level of the back when the animal is running.

The coyote's basic body color ranges from a dull yellow to gray. Coyotes have yellow-colored eyes like foxes, but the eyes of coyote pups differ from those of fox pups by the shape of their pupils. The pupils of coyote pups are round while those of the fox are elliptical.

Depending on location, the mating season occurs between January and March. Although the same coyote pair might breed for many years in a row, they do not mate for life. A coyote pair will set up a territory as their own, breeding, hunting and raising pups there. Coyotes are able to reproduce at 1 year of age.

The gestation period is 60 to 63 days and a litter of five to seven pups is the norm. The pups are born in a concealed den consisting of two or more tunnels leading to a 3- to 4-foot-deep hole in the ground.

Coyotes often enlarge abandoned badger, wood-chuck, fox or skunk burrows for use as dens. They might also use old coyote burrows, or less often, dig a new den. Rock crevices, rocky cliff bases, riverbanks and holes under stumps are also utilized.

The entrance to the den usually measures about 10 inches wide by 13 inches high. One way in which a coyote den might be distinguished from a fox den is by the tidiness inside and around the entrance. Unlike foxes, adult coyotes remove bones and other debris so these materials do not accumulate in or around the edges of the den.

The female will prepare more than one den before the pups are born so that the young can be moved to a safe place if predators threaten, or if fleas become too bothersome.

Pups are born with short, yellow-brown fur. Their eyes open after about 10 days; at this time they can crawl around the den. The male brings

Coyote Range

food to the female while she stays with the pups for the first two months after they are born. Some of this food is regurgitated to feed the pups during and after weaning.

At 3 months old, the pups have been weaned and the den has been abandoned. The pups are taught to hunt by following the parents on hunting trips. By the end of the summer, the pups usually move out of the parents' territories, but sometimes the young coyotes stay with the parents and form a hunting pack.

Coyote pups (right) are born in a concealed den and cared for by both parents. Pups stay close to the den (above) until they are about 3 months old, when they begin following their parents on hunting trips.

HUNTING RED FOXES

The red fox has long been a universal symbol of animal cunning, and throughout history has been the subject of considerable folklore. Fables such as "The Fox and the Crow," "The Fox and the Grapes" and "The Fox and the Woodsman," just to name a few, revere the animal's prowess as a cunning and intelligent trickster.

A glance at any thesaurus will quickly turn up synonyms for "foxy" such as sly, experienced, crafty, knowing, sagacious, wily, astute … the list goes on and on. The fox has long been given attributes that hold it in high esteem.

While the fox is indeed an effective and skillful predator, most fur hunters will tell you that the fox's crafty behavior is actually a product of its incredible senses and paranoid disposition. Its nose. Its eyesight. Its predatory instinct. They all play a part in making the fox the most wary of the medium-sized predators.

It is a matter of survival. Not only must foxes provide a constant supply of food for their families, they must be on vigilant guard against the larger predators that persistently stalk them.

The fox is a member of the canine family, widespread throughout the world, and has historically been of considerable economic importance to man. Its pelt is a valuable staple of the fur industry. During the fur boom of the 1970s and early 1980s, prime fox pelts brought as much as $80 apiece.

A fast runner with a loping speed of about 6 mph and the ability to accelerate to 45 mph for a mile or more when necessary, the fox is known for its expertise in escaping danger.

The red fox is a highly adaptable species. One factor contributing to its successful survival in such widely different habitat is its versatile hunting behavior and varied tastes, which enable it to capitalize on a vast array of prey species.

Fox society is complex and well defined. Throughout most of the year, red foxes are very territorial with the dominant animals occupying the most suitable habitat.

GEARING UP FOR RED FOXES

Guns & Accessories

On average, a red fox weighs about 10 pounds and does not require a lot of killing. Hunters who stalk the prairie grasslands and expansive farmlands of the Dakotas and points west, shoot long-range, fur-friendly calibers like the .17 Rem., .22 Hornet, .222 Rem. and .223 Rem., as well as a preponderance of wildcat calibers designed for optimum accuracy and efficiency. Eastern hunters, who hunt small farms, clear-cuts and swamp edges—typical fox habitat east of the big river—add the popular .22 Win. Mag. rimfire to the list of red fox calibers.

Red foxes prey heavily on rodents during the winter. This fox uses his keen hearing to detect a rodent moving under the snow (top). Proficiently flushing his prey, he pounces on it and then enjoys a tasty meal.

Plastic-tipped bullets (available from many major manufacturers and in most popular calibers), or hollow points provide good fox fodder. They ensure the accuracy needed for small targets, and they keep fur damage to a minimum.

Red foxes invariably circle downwind of the call, often at long range. It's their suspicious nature to do so. Shooting prone provides the best option when cover needed to break up your outline is scarce. I fit my fox rifles with extendible bipods such as those made by Harris Engineering. In their most retracted setting, they hold the scope to eye level while I'm lying flat on the prairie duff, providing a sturdy shooting platform.

Most fox hunters use variable-setting scopes that adjust from around 3X to 10 or 12X. And since the best fox hunting occurs during those dim-light hours just before sunup and just after sundown, large, light-gathering objective lenses are a red fox hunter's best friend. High-quality scopes are a must for serious fox hunting, as are good binoculars for scanning the countryside.

Shotguns work great when hunting in tight cover such as thick edges where red foxes like to stalk their prey. No. 4 or No. 6 shot in a tightly choked 12 gauge is deadly on foxes, and does surprisingly little damage to the fur. Super-tight chokes, like those used on special-purpose turkey guns, provide welcome additional yards of knockdown power.

Calls

I prefer small closed-reed calls and open-reed calls for red foxes—those capable of producing high-pitched bird and rodent sounds. I have found that red foxes are sensitive to loud volume; the softer, higher-pitched tones emitted by these calls seem to appeal to their apprehensive nature. Rest assured, on a calm day a fox will hear even your quietest rodent squeals from a quarter mile away or more.

Electronic callers offer a wide array of sounds that are extremely effective on red foxes. Electronic callers also render discriminating control of volume. There are a great number of squealing bird, rodent and baby rabbit tapes on the market that delight the red fox's senses. For a change-up, try the sounds of red fox pups in distress or territorial barks during the winter breeding season.

Electronic callers offer a wide array of sounds—such as birds, rodents and rabbits—that are effective for calling red foxes.

Red Fox Profile

The "Old World" form of the red fox ranges virtually over all of Europe, temperate Asia and northern Africa. The "New World" red fox inhabits most of North America north of Mexico.

Reddish brown in color, the red fox sports long guard hairs and soft, fine underfur. A long white-tipped tail and black ears and legs accent their beautiful coat. Colors may vary, however. The red fox might appear in several color phases, including black, silver and a mixture of black and red.

A medium-sized predator, the red fox is typically 36 to 42 inches long and weighs about 8 to 15 pounds. In the East, its preferred habitat is mixed farmlands and woodlots where small mammals exist in high numbers. In the central states and the West, the adaptable red fox does well in open prairie country as well as in rougher, rockier places.

Small rodents and birds make up the majority of their diet but when food is scarce,

Red Fox Range

foxes will forage for fruit, eggs and often the carrion of larger animals.

Except during the breeding season, the red fox lives and sleeps in the open even during the bitterly cold winters in its northern range. The fox sleeps with its bushy tail wrapped around the outside of its body. This makes the animal inconspicuous plus allows its warm breath to circulate through the tail fur to protect its sensitive foot pads and nose from frostbite.

Red foxes mate in the winter and produce 1 to 10 offspring the following spring. The pups remain in the den for about five weeks and are cared for by both parents throughout the summer.

Red foxes (above), found throughout most of North America, are well known for their beautiful reddish-orange coat. The 1 to 10 pups born in early spring (right) are cared for by both parents.

The Big Four

STRATEGIES FOR HUNTING RED FOXES

Stand Selection

With red foxes, it is imperative to have good visibility downwind of your calling position. Red foxes invariably circle the source of the sound and use any available cover, even slight breaks in the terrain, when approaching the call. Foxes are most often hunted in open country and a lack of available cover usually requires that you lie low, often in the prone position. If you can gain any elevation, say from sitting in a rock pile or on a slight hill, you will gain precious visibility.

It is advisable to hunt with a partner, positioning the shooter 50 to 100 yards downwind of the caller. This way the shooter will be able to intercept foxes that venture downwind—out of range, and maybe out of sight of the caller. If I am hunting alone, I use an electronic caller with a remote control. This way I can operate the caller from the downwind position and cut the distance between my setup and circling foxes.

Set up with the wind blowing into or across your face. Optimally, the sun should be at your back. Again, make sure you have an open shooting lane downwind of your position, so you have a chance at those foxes that circle downwind.

Calling Sequence

The red foxes I have met have been sensitive to volume. I always begin my calling sequences as though there is a fox hiding within the folds of the cover only 50 yards away. If I get no takers early on, I incrementally increase the volume with each series of calls. I generally blow the tube or play the tape for about 20 to 30 seconds and then remain quiet for about a minute. I give red foxes a little more time to respond to the call because they are more shy than coyotes and often take more time to respond. But I rarely stay at the stand for more than 20 to 25 minutes.

Red foxes like to hunt open hay fields for rodents. Large round bales and grassy fencerows make good hideouts for your ambush.

Night Hunting

Buddy hunting is your best bet when hunting at night, because foxes will often circle downwind out of sight in the safety of the dark. Position the shooter at least 100 yards downwind of the caller. If it is legal to use artificial lights, a red lens will help illuminate a fox's eyes but will rarely spook him. I prefer to hunt by the light of the moon for foxes. Shotguns or .22 rimfires are good choices for night hunting.

Red foxes sleep out in the open and can often be seen curled up in a ball on the downwind side of a hill.

Spotting & Stalking

Red foxes sleep out in the open and can often be seen curled up in a ball on the downwind side of a hill in the warm afternoon sun. A good technique for hunting during the day is to drive around and look for sleeping foxes. Once you find one, devise a stalk, using available cover and keeping the wind in your favor, to get close enough for a setup. Sneak in and call softly to the sleeping fox. If the fox needs a meal more than a nap, it will often respond to the call.

If you find a sleeping fox, you can attempt to stalk to within 100 yards or so and then attempt to call him in.

HUNTING GRAY FOXES

Characteristically, the gray fox is more retiring than its red cousin, and is often perceived as being less crafty and more aggressive by hunters who pursue it. Gray foxes are typically found in forested, rocky and brush-covered country from Canada to northern South America. A native of North America, the gray fox is more plentiful in the temperate climates of the southern United States and Mexico than in the northern reaches of its range.

One of the gray fox's most interesting characteristics is its ability to climb trees, a handy attribute for eluding larger predators and foraging for fruits, insects and mast crops. Gray foxes are rarely found far from heavy cover, where they prey on a wide variety of small animals.

The gray fox varies in appearance east and west. While the Western gray fox is small and slender with silky, thin fur and delicate features, the Eastern gray fox is much stockier and sports a coarse, heavy coat, especially in the North. The coat is usually salt-and-pepper and tinged with rust. The Western gray fox's beautiful coat has traditionally made it more valuable in the fur trade.

In the Southwest, where they are abundant, gray foxes inhabit rock rumbles typical to the transition zone where pinyon-juniper growths rise out of low-lying deserts. Grays are also found in rimrock country and brushy dry washes representative of the high-

12 gauge shotguns loaded with No. 4 shot are deadly on gray foxes and do little fur damage.

desert ecosystem.

In the Deep South and in timbered Northern ranges, gray foxes inhabit wooded or brushy areas, particularly mixed hardwood forests. They typically den in underground burrows, under rocks, in hollow logs or in hollow trees.

While they prefer to hunt through the night, especially in the populated East, gray foxes can be seen foraging for food during the day, though they usually remain close to cover where they can elude their enemies.

GEARING UP FOR GRAY FOXES

Guns & Accessories

Gray foxes, like reds, don't require a lot of firepower, and range is rarely a factor with these hard-charging predators because of the tight cover you are likely to find them in. East or West, the .22 Win. Mag. loaded with jacketed hollow-point bullets, or a 12 gauge loaded with No. 6s or No. 4s, gets the nod every time. The only exception would be if you're calling in terrain where a coyote is just as likely to answer the call. In that case, up your horsepower while trying to remain on the gentle side, with centerfire calibers such as the .17 Rem., .22 Hornet, .222 Rem. or .223 Rem.

With shotguns, it's a little tougher to find a fitting compromise. I've had coyotes run off after receiving a close-range dose of No. 6s. By the same token, the No. 4 buckshot or copper-plated BBs I prefer for coyotes can damage fox pelts. If coyotes are going to be a possibility, your best bet is to go with loads that will effectively anchor coyotes. Then try to keep your shots at foxes limited to those in the 30- to 40-yard range where fur damage will be less extensive.

I consider gray fox pursuit a close-range game,

much like hunting the tom turkey. The object is to experience the thrill of having this bold little predator approach shotgun-close with tail at full mast begging for rabbit. I prefer to rely on my hunting and calling skills to draw the animal within the considerable reach of my tightly choked 12 gauge.

Most gray fox action will be fast and furious, and I usually shoot from a sitting position whether I'm carrying a scattergun or a rifle. For this reason, I prefer low-powered scopes if I'm carrying a rifle. Hunting buddy-style, with one hunter carrying a rifle and the other carrying a shotgun, will increase your odds of having the right tool handy for the job. Some enterprising hunters carry two guns to the stand: a shotgun and a rifle. Many hunters sit with the shotgun in hand for close-range work and the rifle handy for hung-up critters.

Calls

Gray foxes are less sensitive to volume than reds. I use both closed-reed calls and open-reed calls to produce the variety of sounds that gray foxes find

Small closed-reed calls produce the high-pitched sounds that gray foxes can't resist.

intriguing: rabbits, birds, rodents and canine pups in distress, for example. I call much as I would for coyotes, beginning at a moderate volume, and then if nothing shows, increasing the intensity with each sequence.

Electronic callers and the variety of prey and territorial sounds available are extremely effective on gray foxes. I've had days when I couldn't raise a flea with a tube, only to throw in a tape and have instant success. A gray fox pup in distress or a gray fox fight tape provides a good change-up if food-source sounds are not working. With gray foxes, don't be afraid to try something different.

Proficient climbers, gray foxes often utilize trees to elude enemies or to have a look around.

into or across your face. I have found that gray foxes generally come straight to the call and then when they get near the source of the sound, they circle downwind. If you're set up right, the fox should be fully committed, and your shot on its way, before the animal can catch your scent.

STRATEGIES FOR HUNTING GRAY FOXES

Stand Selection

You have to hunt gray foxes where they live and most often that means in tight cover. In the West, navigating the rock rumbles and brush-choked creek-bottoms where they spend the majority of their time is the norm. In the East, hardwood ridges, river-bottoms and transitional zones between swampy areas and heavy timber are good places to find foxes.

Gray foxes favor brush-choked dry washes, where they can escape from larger predators and hunt the many prey species that utilize this habitat.

I look for tight areas with fingers of open shooting lanes that stretch out in several directions. Always have an open lane downwind for those foxes that circle your position.

If I'm hunting an area where there are existing permanent treestands, I might use them to gain precious added visibility. I have found that in the East, particularly, calling from these elevated platforms can be extremely effective.

Always try to set up with the wind blowing

Calling Sequence

Gray foxes approach the call aggressively. Always be on the alert from the first moment you blow the call or turn on the electronic player. I've had gray foxes that were apparently sleeping or hunting nearby show up in seconds, often arriving in pairs.

My calling sequence is similar to what I use for coyotes. I get on the call for about 20 to 30 seconds and then sit quietly for about a minute or more. If I am hunting exclusively for gray foxes, I rarely sit for more than 15 minutes. However, bobcats like to hang out in the same type of terrain and if I have the time and the inclination, I wait it out 30 minutes or more if I think there might be a cat lurking nearby. I always look for sign going to my stands; if I notice fresh cat sign, I will remain longer at the stand.

Night Hunting

Gray foxes are even bolder under the cover of darkness than they are during daylight. A favored technique in Texas, where it is legal to spotlight from a truck, is to call and shoot from a platform mounted atop a 4-wheel-drive truck. Gray foxes will often charge right up to the truck and offer a close-range shot for your scattergun. Those foxes that hang up can be dealt with by using a rifle. Handheld lights, and those mounted atop rifles and shotguns, work well for gray foxes, and battery-operated models can easily be toted to the stand.

Shotguns, .22 Mag. rimfires or the mighty-mouse centerfire rifles get the nod for night hunting.

Gray Fox Profile

A native of North America, the gray fox is typically found in forested, rocky and brush-covered habitat. Though its range stretches from Canada to northern South America, the gray fox is more plentiful in the warm climates of the southern United States and Mexico than in Northern climes.

The gray fox is distinguishable by the reddish color on its neck, ears and legs. It weighs from 7 to 13 pounds and grows to a length of 30 to 40 inches. The gray fox prefers to hunt at night, preying on moles, rabbits, rats, mice, birds, lizards, shellfish and insects. Fruit and other vegetation also make up part of its diet.

*Gray Fox
Range*

Gray foxes usually stay close to their dens, which are typically hidden in the rocks or hollow trees. They mate in early spring in the northern range and in January or February in the South. The pups are born about two months later in an underground den lined with soft shredded bark or dry leaves and grass. Like the young of the red fox, gray fox pups are independent when about 5 months old.

It is believed that gray foxes can live 6 to 10 years in the wild. Their major causes of death include predation, parasites, diseases and man.

Gray foxes are most common in the eastern and southern United States.

The Big Four

HUNTING BOBCATS

*I*f you've ever watched your house cat stalk the small critters that frequent your backyard, you've seen a pretty good example of the hunting style of the bobcat. This sneaker hunts in typical cat fashion, using its incredible eyesight, hearing and speed to locate and capture its prey.

Curious by nature and stealthy by design, it zigzags through its territory investigating objects, inanimate or alive, that catch its attention.

Bobcats are masters of the ambush, as well as skillful stalkers. They often lie in wait of their next meal and pounce with lightning speed when their unsuspecting prey ventures too close. But they are only good for a short burst of speed, and quarry that is missed on the first attack is seldom chased very far.

Native to North America, bobcats number about 1 million and occupy a wide variety of habitats throughout most of the United States. Bobcats are typically found in deep, thick cover. These cats typically avoid human contact, which explains why they are scarce in central farming areas and in much of the urbanized East.

In the West and Southwest, where they are most abundant, bobcats occupy the same rugged terrain that gray foxes favor, and for the same reasons: to avoid larger predators such as coyotes and lions, and to stalk the small animals that live there. These haunts might include brush-choked creekbottoms, deep canyons and ragged rimrock country. In the South, North and East, bobcats prefer forested regions with thick underbrush, occasional clearings, cliffs and timbered swamps. Common den sites include fallen trees, hollow logs, thickets, caves and rock piles.

Bobcats vary in color and size as the geography of their habitat varies. Most bobs sport a coat

that is a mixture of browns, buffs and whites. The fur on their bodies is almost always spotted, but those spots can be inconspicuous, especially on Eastern cats, which are typically muddy brown in color. The bellies on Western cats are snow-white, with prominent black spots creating an elegant pattern. The ears are usually tufted on fully adult bobcats.

GEARING UP FOR BOBCATS

Guns & Accessories

Calling bobcats is generally an in-your-face affair, because of the tight cover where you will find them. East or West, the .22 Win. Mag. loaded with jacketed hollow-point bullets or some of the lighter .22 caliber centerfires such as the .17 Rem., .22 Hornet, .222 Rem. or .223 Rem. are good choices for this animal. While bobcats might exceed 35 pounds and often outweigh many coyotes, they are not nearly as tough to subdue.

For close-up work in tight brush, a tightly choked 10 gauge or 12 gauge loaded with No. 6s or No. 4s will do a dandy job on bobcats. In country that is more open, No. 4 buckshot might be a good option, especially if you'll be shooting at ranges that stretch the length of your barrel.

Rifle hunters generally employ low-powered scopes for close work. Scopes with large objective lenses draw more light and will help extend those precious minutes at dawn and dusk when the bobcat is most likely to be on the prowl.

I often use shooting sticks for bobcat work because I'm generally going to be sitting for a spell and, being a sneaker, the bobcat is unlikely to charge the stand. The steady shot offered by a solid rest helps guarantee more precise bullet placement and decreases the chance of fur damage.

Calls

The bobcats I have met seemed to respond best to the high-pitched sounds of birds and rodents. Small closed-reed or open-reed calls replicate these squeals to a tee. A fawn bleat is another option and there are a number of calls on the market that will produce this sound.

If I opt to go electric, I carry a good supply of bird and rodent sounds, as well as a rabbit or two. In the East, you might consider using the recorded cries of a whitetail fawn in distress as a good change-up. I have also found that the sounds of a gray fox pup in distress will work when other calls fail.

Native to North America, bobcats occupy a variety of habitats throughout most of the United States.

Bobcat Profile

Though they prey mostly on rabbits, hares, birds and rodents, bobcats might also feed on deer and other larger animals.

Secretive and seldom seen in the wild, bobcats inhabit a variety of habitat throughout the United States. Like most members of the feline family, the bobcat stalks its prey, relying on its keen eyesight and hearing.

Males maintain fairly large territories that might cover 50 square miles and overlap the territories of several females. Bobcats rely heavily on rabbits and hares as the mainstay of their diet but might also feed on venison, small birds, mice, squirrels and other small animals. They use their considerable speed in hunting and killing their victims.

Bobcats are about twice the size of a common house cat, standing 20 to 23 inches high at the shoulder and measuring 30 to 35 inches in length. The bobcat gets its name from its short "bobbed" tail that is about 5 to 6 inches in length. Small tufts of hair extend from the tips of the ears, making them look pointed, and a ruff of long fur that extends along the cheekbones gives the bobcat's face a full, rounded appearance.

Bobcat Range

Strategies for Hunting Bobcats

Stand Selection

As I mentioned, you will find bobcats where they live: in the meanest cover available. This usually translates to rough rock-strewn areas and brush-choked creekbottoms in the West and Southwest, and hardwood ridges, riverbottoms, swamps and transitional timber throughout the rest of their range.

Look for openings along the edges of heavy cover and try to pull the cat out to you. Keep a close watch! A bobcat will take advantage of every smidgen of cover to close the distance between itself and its prey. Bobcats hunt by sight, so wind direction is less of a consideration than it would be if you were hunting canines.

If I'm hunting hilly areas, I call from an elevated position for added visibility. I often set up with an obstruction behind me, like a sharp cliff, so that I can better predict which direction the cat is most likely to approach from.

Calling Sequence

If you're going to play the cat-and-mouse game, you'll need the patience of Job. Many hunters have the false notion that bobcats do not respond aggressively or consistently to the call, or that they are call-shy. Failure to call in cats is more a function of population density and the animal's hunting style than an absence of calling skills.

Bobcats are generally less abundant than canine predators and often occupy larger territories. They also take their merry time coming to the call. This means the chance of sitting down within earshot of bobcats is statistically lower than when hunting, say, coyotes. You have some control over where you set up, but you must remain on the stand long enough for the cat to respond.

I generally begin with low volume, as I would with canines. Bobcats have keen ears and if they are close, I don't want to blow them out of the country. Cats, I believe, require a little more coaxing than canines

Bobcats are sneakers and come to the call more slowly than canines. To be successful, plan on staying put on your stand for 30 or more minutes.

and seem to be easily distracted from the call. For this reason, I take shorter breaks between my calling sequences when I'm targeting cats. The same with electronic callers. I run the tape more frequently or might even let it play continuously.

I remain on the stand a minimum of 30 minutes. Cats are sneaky loafers. You must be patient and give them time to respond.

Night Hunting

Bobcats are most active at night and during those magic minutes just before sundown and just prior to sunup. Daylight movement is rare except during the late winter breeding season, when they are stretching the boundaries of their territories in search of mates.

In the North, I like to hunt bobcats during the winter by the light of the moon. Setting up in clearings and calling to the edges of heavy cover can be productive. Be patient. Bobcats will likely hang up, in typical cat fashion, and ponder the situation long and hard before committing to the call and breaking cover, even at night.

Shotguns, .22 Mag. rimfires or dainty centerfire calibers are your best bets when working the graveyard shift for bobcats.

Bobcats are highly nocturnal, and many hunters go to work when the sun is sinking low.

Chapter Six

HUNTING
OTHER CRITTERS

A ny book written on the topic of predator hunting would be incomplete without a discussion about some of the other animals that sometimes come to the hunter's call. In many areas of the West, those unexpected visitors might include lions, black bears and raccoons. In regions east of the Mississippi, populations of raccoons and black bears are abundant, and hunting opportunities for both species exist.

Due to a sharp decline in fur prices in recent years, trapping pressure on raccoons has dipped dramatically. In much of the Midwest, South and East, raccoon populations are exploding and opportunities to hunt them are relatively unexploited. Hunters willing to knock on a few doors in agricultural areas will find no shortage of places to hunt raccoons.

Black bear numbers are increasing throughout most regions of the United States and the opportunity to hunt them has never been better. Licenses in many states are allocated by lottery draws, but as bear numbers have increased the chances of obtaining a license have also increased. While it might be considered a low percentage undertaking, using predator calls to hunt black bears is effective under the right conditions and provides unmatched excitement and challenge.

Though lions can be successfully called to the tube, the number taken compared to other predators is low because of the vast territories these elusive animals occupy and because of their suspicious nature. However, the excitement of a close encounter of the lion kind makes it a popular pursuit, if not an obsession, with some callers. Venturing into the rugged rimrock terrain preferred by the big cats will test the mettle of even the most determined predator hunter.

Predator hunters looking to extend their hunting seasons or simply to face new and exciting challenges will benefit from calling the uncalled. Hunters who primarily pursue the "Big Four" can add to the adventure of calling predators by expanding their boundaries to include not-so-often-called critters—raccoons, black bears and lions.

HUNTING RACCOONS

Often referred to as the "masked bandit" for its deviant appearance and thieving ways, the raccoon is abundant throughout most of North America. Rarely found far from water, raccoons prefer habitat that includes streams, rivers, ponds, marshes or lakes.

The raccoon's lifestyle revolves around its stomach, and the animals spend a considerable amount of time and energy building up fat reserves for their low activity time in winter. Contrary to common belief, the raccoon does not hibernate, but during extremely cold weather in Northern climes, it might stay denned up for weeks at a time. In Southern states, raccoons typically remain active throughout the winter.

If it's edible, chances are that raccoons will consume it. Primary food sources include crayfish, frogs, salamanders, earthworms, fruits, nuts, grains, carrion, eggs and any available small mammals and birds.

Raccoons are nocturnal by nature and are rarely seen during the day, when they are vulnerable to larger predators.

GEARING UP FOR RACCOONS

Guns & Accessories

Raccoon hunting is a nighttime affair, providing close-up encounters. Raccoons are slow and methodical compared to canines and felines, and relatively easy to subdue; .22 Long Rifle or .22 Win. Mag. rimfires and shotguns are your best bets for hunting the masked bandit.

A hollow-point bullet through the chest will usually drop a raccoon on the spot with little fur damage. But even though action is likely to be of a close-range nature, raccoons are constantly on the move, so shots at moving targets are the norm. It's a good idea to practice snap off-hand shots before venturing afield for raccoons. In the West, where hunters generally hunt from the tops of vehicles, rimfires are the perfect tool for coons.

Shotguns loaded with 1 1/4 oz. of No. 6 or No. 4 copper-plated shot are lethal and fur-friendly. Scatterguns are a good call for raccoons when hunting areas with lots of coons, where multiple animals might show up on short notice. Action can be fast and frantic.

Calls

Raccoons respond best to the sounds of their own kind. I prefer young coon-in-distress and fighting coon tapes powered by an electronic player.

Raccoon Profile

Raccoons are abundant throughout most of the North American continent and are easily identified by a black face mask and bushy tail with alternating black and light-colored rings. Racoons can be found in all types of habitat, but are most abundant in and on the edges of urban and suburban areas where there is a mixture of farmland and woodlots and agricultural crops. Coons are also fond of rivers, ponds and lakeshores, where they search for such food as small fish, snails, earthworms, clams, crayfish and other aquatic animals. Other favorite foods include persimmons, wild grapes and plums, blackberries and acorns, just to name a few.

Raccoon Range

Raccoons are prolific and breed with several different mates. Breeding occurs from January through March, and one litter of three to four young is typical. The young begin venturing out of the den at 30 to 60 days of age and will accompany their mother on extended trips by the time they are 8 to 10 weeks old. Young raccoons are self-sufficient by fall but often remain with their mother until the next spring, when her next litter is born.

Find corn and water, and you'll most assuredly find raccoons. Hunt the edges of urban and suburban areas where you find a mixture of streams, woodlots and agricultural crops.

Hunting Other Critters

Since most raccoon hunting occurs after dark, handheld lights like these are used to locate them.

Tubes will work for calling raccoons but with less frequency. So if at all possible, go electric for coons. Food-source sounds that work for coons include rodents and various birds in distress.

Lights

Good lighting equipment is crucial to a productive night of coon hunting, and thankfully there is no shortage of good lighting products on the market that are specifically designed for working the dark. Most hunters use handheld lights, with intensity controls and removable red and amber lenses for locating coons, and bright white lights mounted to the top of the gun at the point of kill. Coal-miner-type lights mounted to a cap, like those used by houndsmen, also work and keep your hands free.

STRATEGIES FOR HUNTING RACCOONS

Stand Selection

Finding raccoons involves finding their food sources, and in the fall that generally means hunting in close proximity to agricultural fields, especially corn, and to water sources. Be mindful: Racoons stay relatively close to their denning areas, so be on the lookout for old hollow trees, abandoned farm buildings and other areas where coons might be hiding during the day.

There's little need to venture far from your vehicle when setting up for coon hunting. In fact, Western hunters hunt from atop their trucks where that's legal. Raccoons show very little fear at night and will regularly approach vehicles to investigate the source of the call sounds.

Selecting productive locations is important, as is timing. Coons move from one food source to another during the course of the night as well as throughout the autumn. They might work an apple orchard for a few nights and then abandon it and move to a cornfield a mile or more away for a few nights. Food sources change throughout the fall so you must constantly monitor raccoons' travel and feeding patterns during those months.

Calling Sequence

Raccoons fearlessly respond to the call. I leave the electronic player on and concentrate on operating the light so that I'm prepared when they show up. I begin with low volume so I don't frighten off any animals that might be hanging close by, and then I increase the volume throughout the stand. I rarely stay longer than 20 minutes at a setup if I haven't spotted any eyes.

The Drive-By

Raccoon hunting is a percentage game, and the more area you can cover in a night the higher your odds will be that you'll come in contact with your target. Once you have secured permission to hunt a piece of property, or better yet several adjoining properties, drive around the area during daylight and become familiar with locations that are likely to hold the most interest for coons—particularly possible denning sites and places where waterways meet agricultural crops.

During a full night of calling, be prepared to make 15 or 20 stops; have as many of them preselected as possible. And throughout the course of the night don't hesitate to call the same locations more than once. If you don't get a response the first time, it might simply mean that the coons haven't gotten there yet.

HUNTING BLACK BEARS

The black bear can best be described as a large and furry food processor. Its entire existence seemingly revolves around where it's going to procure its next meal. And more than any other big game animal, black bears can be found camped out at specific food sources at specific times of the year.

This inherent characteristic suggests that to hunt black bears successfully you must locate (or create) their food sources. Where it's legal, baiting is one of the most effective means of bringing hunter and bear together. Another favored tactic is hunting them with the use of hounds where that's legal.

You should know that calling black bears using food-source sounds is difficult at best. It requires a combination of good woodsman skills, solid hunting tactics and a great deal of luck. Results are far from predictable, as they often are with smaller predators.

Bears might take a long time to come to the call and then charge in aggressively at the last moment. Or they might come methodically to the call only to veer off and wander in another direction. And bears are simply not as abundant as smaller canine or feline predators: The chances of a close encounter are slim at best.

But before you become disenchanted, remember that the stakes have been raised. The excitement and sense of accomplishment of successfully calling in and killing this magnificent predator are worth the price of admission.

Those hunters who wish to take the predator game to a higher level will accept the black bear challenge. Here are a few tips to help you along that road.

GEARING UP FOR BLACK BEARS

Guns & Accessories

Consider first that we're talking about a potentially dangerous animal that can weigh several hundred pounds and has the weaponry, if not the inclination, to rip you into pieces.

143

Black Bear Profile

Black bears are numerous and widespread throughout North America, with a population estimated somewhere between 400,000 and 750,000. Their range stretches from the northern arctic south throughout most of Canada and the United States.

Comfortable living in close proximity to man, black bears prefer habitats that include heavy forests broken by occasional open areas such as clear-cuts, meadows and agricultural fields. This includes hardwood forests in the East as well as the coniferous forests found in the more central and western regions of the continent. Home ranges usually revolve around a number of small food sources connected by travel ways. The travel ranges of males are much larger than those of females, sometimes encompassing up to 50 square miles.

Black Bear Range

Black bears can weigh as much as 600 pounds or more, but more typically average 150 to 250 pounds. Individual variation in weight is generally a reflection of genetics, food availability and climatic conditions. Bears eat practically anything they can find and, generally, more than 75 percent of their diet consists of vegetable matter such as nuts, berries, agricultural crops, grasses and roots. However, bears will also feed on the carrion of other animals, fish, birds, small mammals and deer fawns.

Female black bears typically mature at 3 to 5 years of age and will mate with several males over the two- or three-week-long breeding season, which occurs in May or June in their Southern territories and as late as July or August in Northern climes. Most black bears, including those that live in moderate climates, hibernate for 4 to 7 months each year, during which time they lose 15 to 30 percent of their body weight. Pregnant sows give birth to up to four tiny cubs during their hibernation the winter following the summer breeding season. Virtually helpless, the cubs can move enough to suckle on their sleeping mother until she awakens in the spring.

Black bear populations are increasing throughout most of their range. Today there are an estimated 400,000 to 750,000 bears in North America.

Using bait can ensure that bears are in the area. By positioning yourself between a bedding area and an active bait station (below), you can intercept a bear (right) on the way to its nightly donut shop visit.

Next, realize that you'll be hiding in the underbrush and imitating the sounds of a free lunch. You should quickly make the connection that a big gun that launches a big bullet is appropriate for black bears. Centerfire calibers capable of pushing 140- to 200-grain bullets make good sense for bears. Calibers falling between the .270 Win. and the .300 Mag. will provide the muscle you want for these bruisers.

Bears have thick hides and carry lots of fat so they usually don't leave a very good blood trail. Good bullet placement is critical. Take great care to make your first shot count, and always try to penetrate both lungs. A bear hit through both lungs will rarely get very far before it expires.

Calls

You'll need a good pair of lungs to call black bears with a mouth call. Bears can be slow to respond and often lose interest quickly between calling sequences. The caller using a tube will likely blow himself dizzy before a bear arrives. For this reason, those who call

bears generally go electric and let the player run continuously.

Keep a close eye out for even the most subtle movement. The sound of the call will likely drown out any audio warning of the bear's arrival. The best sounds for bears are those that ring the dinner bell. A bleating fawn, rabbits in distress, domestic livestock such as pigs or goats in distress, and even the distress cries of various birds, are all good choices.

STRATEGIES FOR HUNTING BLACK BEARS

Importance of Scouting

To have a chance at a black bear you need to do your homework, and that translates into plenty of advanced scouting. Look for scat, tracks, overturned rocks, dug-up anthills, decaying logs and other evidence of bear activity. Look for trails through thickets or swamps. Find regular food sources and determine routes to and from bedding areas. The more you can learn about bear densities and travel patterns prior to calling, the better your chances will be of calling in a bruin.

Spotting & Calling

Bears can respond to the call lethargically, and anything you can do to intercept them on their line of travel will increase your odds of getting close enough for a shot. In the wide-open expanses of the

Though black bears prey on white-tailed fawns in early spring, calls that imitate a fawn in distress are effective any time of year.

West, where bears are likely to be found along the edges of heavy cover, spotting and stalking in tandem with calling might be your best bet.

Find an elevated vantage point and glass the countryside until you find a bear. Your scouting has already indicated that there are bears in the area, and you should have a pretty good understanding of their travel patterns between feeding and bedding areas. Once you spot a bear, try to determine its travel route and attempt to intercept the bear. Set up and call for at least an hour. It is easier to pull a bear to the source of the sound if it's already heading in that direction.

Baiting

Bait stations can be used in conjunction with calling and can increase the odds that there's a bear within earshot of your efforts.

Using a call near your bait station may bring a bear in earlier than usual, while there's still plenty of shooting light.

By positioning yourself between a bedding area and an active bait station, you can intercept bears on the way to their nightly visit to the donut shop.

Bears move to food-source locations late in the evening and complete most of their feeding at night. Talk to any hunter who has perched over a bait station and he will likely tell you that bears most often show up within an hour or so of darkness. By intercepting bears on the way to the bait station, you have a little more time to play with. Settle in with your electronic player and give the bears a good hour to respond before you switch locations. If you've done a good job of scouting, your efforts should put a bear within hearing distance of the call. The rest is up to the bear.

HUNTING MOUNTAIN LIONS

ost North American predator hunters probably consider the mountain lion, or cougar, the ultimate trophy. The difficulties and dangers associated with hunting this large feline make it a challenge that all but the most hardened predator hunters avoid. Solitary by nature and inherently dangerous, this animal can easily turn the hunter into the hunted.

Cougar numbers are on the rise throughout the cat's Western range, and the chance of calling one in, although slim, has never been better. In Colorado alone, the lion population is estimated at 2,000 to 4,000 animals.

It is still legal to hunt lions in many of the Western states, but public sentiment and aggressive anti-hunting campaigns waged by animal-rights activists have led to the protection of the animal in some states, and this has created increased human/lion encounters and increased attacks on domestic livestock and pets.

California, for example, gave cougars full protection in 1972, when hunting them was banned. Current California law, set by a ballot measure back in 1990, makes it illegal to kill a mountain lion except in self-defense or after wildlife officials have issued a permit to kill a lion that has attacked livestock or pets.

Prior to 1990, there had been no recorded fatalities from cougar attacks in California. However, as of this printing, there have been six cougar attacks on people since 1990, including two fatal attacks on women joggers. There were also 322 mountain lion attacks on pets and livestock recorded in one year alone. It is estimated that the statewide mountain lion population grew from fewer than 3,000 in the early 1970s to between 4,000 and 6,000 recently.

Lions have few natural enemies, so the only means of controlling their population is by regulated harvest, which includes hunting and trapping. Hopefully, Western game agencies will continue to manage these large cats using methods based on scientific fact and will turn a deaf ear, as much as possible, to animal-rights rhetoric that has little basis in reality.

GEARING UP FOR LIONS

Guns & Accessories

The lion is a sneaker, like most felines, and often shows up unannounced. Your choice of firearm should reflect the fact that you're hunting a large, potentially dangerous animal—one that is stalking you if your best calling efforts have convinced it that something good to eat is waiting just ahead.

Adult lions generally weigh from about 70 to 160 pounds and most of the calibers favored by Western hunters, from .22-250 Rem. up, are lethal on these big cats.

It is sensible to carry a quick-handling rifle that you are intimately familiar with, should a quick second shot become necessary.

Variable-power scopes are probably a good choice when hunting the big country that cats favor. Although you should keep the scope set at its lowest setting should a lion show up without warning, the added magnification

might come in handy if you get a sneaker that holds up a couple of football fields away. I always carry shooting sticks when hunting the West. A solid rest for long-range shots is a prerequisite to success.

Calls

Lions will respond to a wide variety of food-source sounds and will do so in a cat-like manner: slow and stealthy. The distress cries of most prey species will work well on the big cats.

Open- or closed-reed tubes that imitate rabbits or birds in distress, or that emulate a deer fawn in distress, are effective on lions as are many of the food-source recordings used on other predators. These recordings include sounds of rabbits, hares, baby pigs, birds and fawns.

Mountain lions inhabit the obtrusive rimrock country of the West, where humans seldom travel.

STRATEGIES FOR HUNTING MOUNTAIN LIONS

Hunt for Sign

Hunting for lions begins by hunting for sign. Population densities are relatively low, and lion territories cover miles of rugged terrain. For this reason, you need to do a little homework to turn the odds of an encounter in your favor.

For a start, talk to ranchers about livestock kills and lion sightings. Also talk to wildlife officers about known lion territories or denning sites. If you are lucky enough to locate a fresh kill—typically lions scatter debris over their kills and revisit the kills until they've been consumed— you've increased your

To hunt lions successfully, begin by scouting for sign. Talk to ranchers about livestock kills or any recent lion sightings.

chances of getting close to a lion. Watch for tracks and scat as you hike from one stand to the next.

The Waiting Game

Like most cats, lions can be slow to respond to the call; your stand selection and patience should reflect their hunting style. Select an elevated position where you have good visibility, and plan to stay there for a good hour or more. I suggest that you back yourself up against a boulder or other large obstruction so that there is little chance that a lion will surprise you from the back door. Select a position where you have some control over the direction from which the lion will approach.

Call every 5 or 10 minutes and then sit quietly, waiting for a response. Scan the terrain with binoculars to pick out any movement on the landscape.

Get into the Outback

Lions prefer rugged country far from the encroachment of human predators, and you can plan on wearing out a little shoe leather if you want to get into prime cat country. Deep brushy canyons, rugged rimrock and mountain foothills make up a large portion of the lion's lair in the West. Figure on trailing off the beaten path if you're going to hunt lions.

Mountain Lion Profile

Once distributed throughout North America, the mountain lion is now primarily a Western resident, although sightings are made each year east of the Mississippi. A small population still exists in southern Florida, where the species is considered endangered. The mountain lion has the widest distribution of any wildcat, ranging from Canada to South America.

Known also by such names as cougar, puma, panther and catamount, the mountain lion is generally a reddish to buff color with a paler underside. Its black-tipped tail extends nearly 3 feet.

Mountain Lion Range

Reported Sightings

Plentiful throughout most of its Western range, lions prefer habitats where deer are abundant and humans are sparse. Deep canyons, obtrusive rimrock, mountain foothills and mesas typical of the West suit the lion's reclusive lifestyle.

Lions are solitary and secretive. A mountain lion is big, so it needs a big home range. An adult male's home range often spans more than 100 square miles and overlaps the ranges of several females. Both male and female lions prey on a variety of animals including deer, wild hogs, jackrabbits, javelinas and rodents. A study on lion feeding habits conducted in Idaho concluded that lions there killed an average of one deer per week, or about 50 annually. They have also been known to kill domestic livestock.

Female lions mate for the first time when they are 2 or 3 years old and the gestation period lasts about 90 days. Up to 6 cubs are born with closed eyes that open fully by the end of the second week. The care of the cubs lies solely with the mother, who brings them food and teaches them to hunt. Male lions are a danger to the youngsters and often attack and kill them if given the chance.

Mountain lions are one of North America's largest predators, weighing as much 200 pounds.

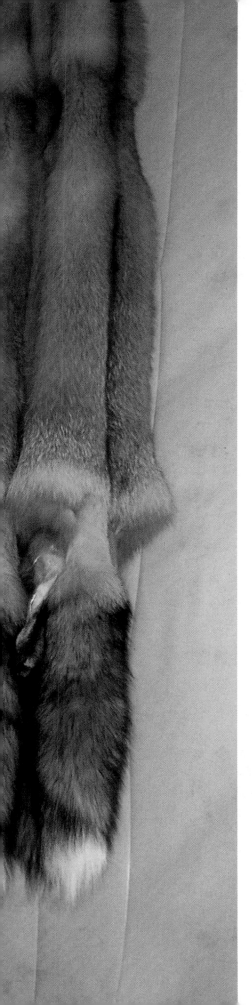

Chapter Seven

THE FUR MARKET

For more than two centuries, the fur trade was the major catalyst for exploration of the North American continent. Craftsmen fashioned the first steel traps more than 500 years ago, and European settlers brought foothold traps to America as early as the 1650s. By the early 1800s, the American fur trade was in full swing, and adventurous men of every description were forging their way into the "New World" seeking fame and fortune.

Frontier trappers would vanish into the wilderness with meager supplies to trap beavers and other furbearing animals in the virgin streams and rivers. In good beaver country, they would take several animals a day, skinning them on the spot. Beaver meat made up the lion's share of their diet.

Back at camp, trappers would scrape, flesh and stretch the skins, then hang them to dry. In the spring, trappers would gather for the annual rendezvous, where they would sell their pelts, socialize with reckless abandon and restock supplies before returning to the mountains.

From its incarnation, the fur industry has dictated the relative value of all furbearing animals, including the predatory species we hunt. Cyclic in nature, this volatile market has seen constant fluctuations. Most recently, the market has experienced a downturn—the result of changes in fashion, unseasonably mild winters domestically and economic upheaval abroad. Pale coyotes and red foxes that demanded $80 to $100 in the late 1970s and early '80s are more likely to bring only $12 to $20 as this book goes to press.

This lull in the market has had a dual effect on our sport. The bad news is that the value of fur is diminished. Gone are the days when a man could make an honest day's wage with a rifle in one hand and a favorite tube call in the other.

The good news? There are more critters to hunt than ever before, and competition for rich fur hunting areas is greatly reduced. Landowners overrun by unwanted critters are opening their doors to predator hunters, and free access has never been easier to obtain.

Even at today's prices, fur is a valuable renewable resource—a just reward for a successful day afield. And there is nothing more awe-inspiring than a collection of prime, finished pelts. Whether you are an avid predator hunter or a casual participant in the sport, your work is incomplete until you've spent that final hour in the fur shed putting up your harvest.

HANDLING YOUR FUR

Caring for your fur begins in the field immediately after a successful hunt. Whether you plan to put up the fur yourself or drop it off at the local fur buyer or taxidermist, a little care in the field will ensure that you get the most out of your pelts.

Take care to keep your animals as clean as possible in the field. That means keeping blood, dirt and other debris from further contaminating the pelt. Stop by a stream, river or other water source and give the fur a quick rinsing. Carry paper towels to plug up wound channels and to wipe excess blood from the mouth, nose and ears. The entire animal can then be dropped off at the fur buyer or taxidermist.

If you have the time and inclination, rough skinning your animals in the field is the best way to ensure that they make it to the fur buyer in the best possible shape. All this requires is a sharp knife, a piece of rope for hanging the animal and a rudimentary understanding of how to peel the hide from the critter. Once the animal is skinned, roll the hide up, fur side out, from nose to tail, and place the package in a clean zip-top bag. Later, the pelt can be frozen if needed until you have time to flesh and stretch it.

Bobcats, foxes, coyotes and raccoons are all case-skinned. This means that the pelt is not slit down the middle but is opened across the hind legs and removed from the carcass in tubular fashion. Canines and felines are stretched with the fur on the outside, while raccoons are stretched with the fur on the inside.

Putting Up Your Fur

The instructions that begin on the next page will give you a basic understanding of how to put up your fur. For more detailed information, talk to your local fur buyer or purchase one of the many good books or videos on the market that explain the process in great detail.

To do a good job, there are a number of tools you will need to complete the skinning and fleshing process: skinning gambrel or length of rope, sharp skinning knife, tail puller and slitter (optional), fur brush, fleshing beam, fleshing tool and a stretching board or wire. It is also a good idea to wear latex gloves to protect yourself from diseases carried by some furbearers.

Preparing a Pelt

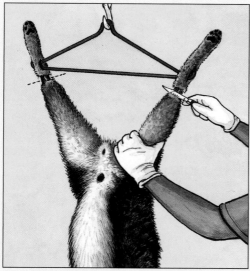

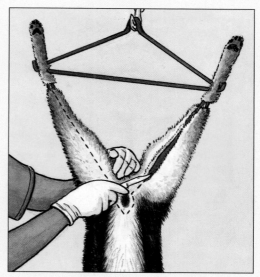

1 To begin, hang the animal by its back legs using a gambrel or length of rope. Use a fur brush, the kind you would use on your dog, to clean dirt and burrs from the fur. With a sharp knife, cut around the ankles on the hind legs as shown, as well as around the elbows of the front legs.

2 From the ankle, cut down the back of the leg slightly on the inside all the way down to the anus. Cut around the anus and back up the other side. Pull the skin away from the hind legs until you get to the tail.

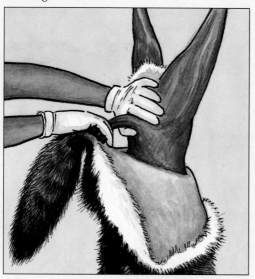

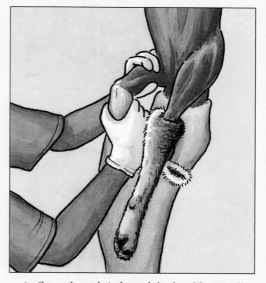

3 Work the skin away from the base of the tail; use your knife, if necessary. Place the tail bone between two fingers and pull the entire bone out of the tail skin. Commercial tail strippers or wooden clothespins make this task easier. Split the tail down to the tip on the middle of the pelt's underside so it can be held open during the drying process to prevent spoiling.

4 Once the pelt is free of the hind legs, pull the skin down away from the carcass using steady pressure until you get to the shoulders. Push your fingers between the front of the shoulder and the pelt. Grab the leg with one hand and the pelt with the other. Pull the leg up while you pull the pelt down at the same time. The leg should easily pull through. Repeat on the other side.

Continued ...

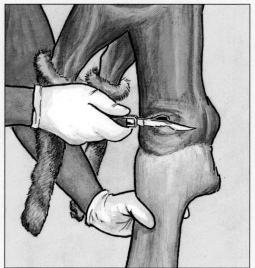

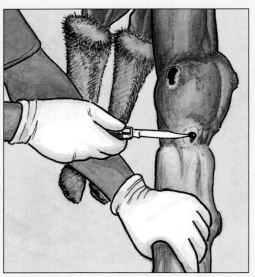

5 Now you're getting to the tricky part—the head. Use your knife to skin around the neck down to the ears. The ears are not always easily visible and you might have to feel around to find them. Cut the ear cartilage close to the skull so the ears come off with the pelt.

6 Continue skinning down until you come to the eyes. Skin the eyes out using the tip of your knife. Take your time here; be careful not to cut the eye openings any larger than their natural size.

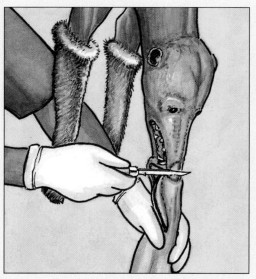

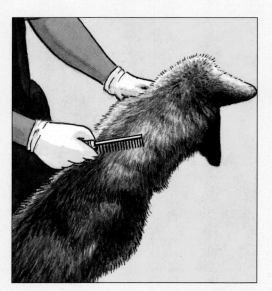

7 Using your knife, skin down to the mouth and separate the lips and nose from the carcass. The nose cartilage should remain attached to the pelt. The lower jaw skin can be removed from the pelt. The pelt is now free from the carcass.

8 This is a good time to wash any blood and dirt from the pelt using cold water. Comb out any remaining burrs and foreign objects that might create a small lump that the fleshing knife might cut through.

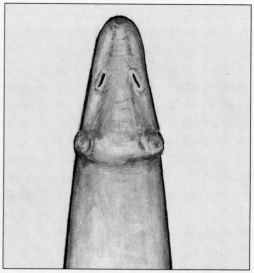

9 Place the pelt on a fleshing beam, belly side up, and with a dull two-handled fleshing knife scrape any fat off the pelt from the chin down the length of the belly. Once the fat is removed from the belly, flip the pelt over and do the same on the back and sides. Remove excess fat around the ears, and flesh out the tail as well. Wipe off any excess grease with a dry rag.

10 Initially, stretch all the animals with the fur to the inside. Raccoons will remain with the fur on the inside, but canine and cat pelts will be flipped over when they are dry to the touch. Center the pelt on the stretcher with the nose on the top in the middle of the board or frame and pull the hide down firmly on the stretcher. Pin open the tail so that it can dry properly.

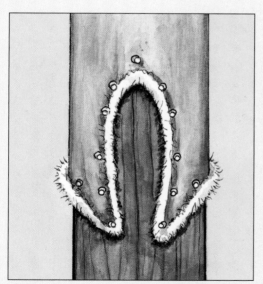

11 Trim around the "window" of the pelt to give it a finished look.

12 The pelt is now ready for drying. Hang it by the nose and dry at room temperature for several days. It is now ready for tanning or to take to the fur buyer.

MARKETING YOUR FUR

ur has long been a world-wide symbol of wealth, affluence, fame and power. Since the early days of the North American fur trade, the industry has thrived in relation to domestic and foreign economic prosperity as well as to fluctuations in fashion and appeal. And while raw fur prices have been relatively flat in recent years, make no mistake about it, there are profitable outlets for the furs you harvest.

Trappers and fur hunters have a number of marketing options, ranging from selling unskinned carcasses to the local fur buyer, to offering finished pelts for sale at local and international fur auctions.

THE LOCAL FUR BUYER

The most popular and widely exercised option for marketing fur is selling finished pelts to a local fur buyer. This is especially true of hunters who only put up a few furs each season and are willing to compromise profit for convenience.

A fur buyer is also a good outlet for hunters who simply want to drop off the animal on the carcass. Most fur buyers will buy "green" pelts (those skinned but not fleshed) and fur on-the-carcass at a reduced rate. They will prepare the animals for market and make the profit on putting up the fur. If you want to get rid of whole animals, this is really your only option.

Local buyers are also excellent sources of information for hunters who wish to put up their own fur but don't have a great deal of experience. Most fur buyers will gladly share tips on handling fur. Many also sell fur handling equipment.

And the reward is immediate. If you are satisfied with the buyer's offer, he will write you a check on the spot and you are on your way. Be warned, though: It is your responsibility to have an idea of what your fur is worth. If you don't believe the offer is fair, don't be afraid to tell him so or to walk away if you are not satisfied.

LOCAL FUR AUCTIONS

Many state and local trappers associations hold annual fur auctions that attract fur buyers from all over the state. The good news is that you are likely to receive competitive prices for your furs at these auctions because of the competition between buyers. The bad news is that you will likely have to pay seller fees or a commission. Depending on the state or organization, it might range from 8 percent to as much as 15 percent. This fee will be deducted from your check upon the sale of your fur.

Your local conservation officer or wildlife agency should be able to tell you how to contact the trappers association in your state. Or, if you know a local trapper, there is a good chance that he already belongs to an association. He might be able to provide information about local auctions.

INTERNATIONAL FUR AUCTIONS

These huge auctions draw potential buyers from all around the world and are excellent outlets if you have a good collection of prepared fur. North American Fur Auctions, Inc. (formerly the Hudson's Bay Company) is the largest fur auctioning facility in the world, processing millions of furs each year. Here, brokers from various nations bid on collections of fur to fill orders they have taken in their home countries.

Typically, trappers and fur hunters in the United States cannot ship fur directly to Canada, but must go through customs brokers who will take care of the necessary paperwork to get the furs over the border.

For information on shipping your furs to an auction in Canada, contact your state's trappers association to locate brokers who will ship your furs for you.

MORE OPTIONS

There are some trappers and fur hunters who take a more entrepreneurial approach to marketing their fur. Some sell to taxidermists who buy whole animal carcasses, mount a full animal and sell them to their customers. Bobcats, for instance, can often bring a better price at the taxidermist than on the fur market. Granted, this is a relatively small outlet, but one worth examining when fur prices are low.

Other hunters market bleached skulls, tanned hides, claws, teeth, tanned tails and other animal parts at flea markets, mountain man rendezvous and trapping conventions. Still others make gloves, hats, ear warmers and all sorts of items from tanned hides and give them away as gifts or sell them.

So you see, the fur that you harvest has economic and social value. It is a valuable renewable resource that allows you to spend more time in the field hunting each year, and it even provides compensation for your efforts.

International fur auctions are a good option for trappers and fur hunters who put up large collections of fur.

INDEX

Index